Jayne Sterne lives in London with her husband and four children. *Destroyed* is her first book.

# JAYNE STERNE

# Destroyed

headline
review

First published in 2008
by HEADLINE REVIEW
An imprint of Headline Publishing Group

First published in paperback in 2008
by HEADLINE REVIEW

1

Cataloguing in Publication Data is available from the British Library

978 0 7553 1799 8

Typeset in Dante by Avon DataSet Ltd,
Bidford-on-Avon, Warwickshire

Printed in the UK by CPI Mackays, Chatham, ME5 8TD

Headline's policy is to use papers that are natural, renewable and recyclable
products and made from wood grown in sustainable forests. The logging and
manufacturing processes are expected to conform to the environmental
regulations of the country of origin.

HEADLINE PUBLISHING GROUP
An Hachette Livre UK Company
338 Euston Road
London NW1 3BH

www.headline.co.uk
www.hachettelivre.co.uk

'The monsters of our childhood do not fade away . . .'

John le Carré

# Contents

# Author's Note

Many of the events described in this book occurred as the result of the unspeakable actions of various individuals. Some of those involved in, or close to, these events are still alive, and I have been advised that several of these people cannot be identified for legal reasons. As a result I have been obliged to conceal the identity of certain characters in the book. At no point, however, have I altered or exaggerated the facts of what happened to me.

# Prologue:

## Night-time

It is the darkness I remember most of all. The darkness and the strangeness of it all.

I am eight years old and lying in my bed. Mum and Dad are asleep. My brothers, Sean and Stuart, are asleep. My little sister, Mandy, is asleep. All around me is pitch-black, and I am huddled under my covers hoping that they will protect me from the hidden terrors of the dark. Night-times have always been scary for me. Bad things happen at night. Things that shouldn't happen.

But tonight I can't sleep, and morning seems a long way away. I am in a strange room in a strange house. The people I am with are strangers and I don't like it here. My mum tucked me in a long time ago, gave me a kiss on my forehead, and whispered, 'Good night, Jayne.' But I have been awake ever since, a jumble of confused thoughts going round in my head. I have been thinking of home, of the life I left behind. And I have been thinking about how happy all the other children seem to be. There will be a party in two days' time, with dressing-up, and music, and cakes. The others are filled with excitement, and I wish I could share it, but somehow I can't.

Something isn't right. It's not just that I find myself in a new place, far away from the life I know so well. There is something else. Some*one* else. His name is Graham. He has red hair and piercing green eyes that seem to see right through me. The grown-ups like him: they like the way he talks to them, and the way he acts with us children. But I am not so sure. I am too little to speak up, to have an opinion about such things, but I don't understand why he always seems to *be* there. When I walk into a room, he is waiting for me. When I try to find somewhere to be alone, he turns up like a bad penny, disturbing me with some made-up question or errand. Occasionally he touches me, and my flesh creeps when he does. I hate it so much.

When the grown-ups are around he goes out of his way to help them, and talks to me in that cheerful, friendly, encouraging voice. Now and then, however, when no one else can see, I catch him looking at me. I don't like the expression in his eyes. There is a deadness there. A flatness. But when it is just me and him, he changes. He becomes scary. He shouts at me, tells me I am stupid, that I am annoying and clumsy and that I am doing things wrong. That I am naughty and will upset my parents. It makes me want to cry, and sometimes I do – though not when the grown-ups are around. It would make them ask what was wrong, and I know I won't be believed even if I find the words for these feelings that I don't understand.

I close my eyes tightly, praying for sleep to come, to extinguish my worries and make me feel safe again. And eventually it does, but not before I am forced to look at his face in my mind's eye, to hear his voice echo in my head.

If I had known what he had in his mind, I would never have fallen asleep that night. I would never have been *able* to fall asleep. I would have run straight into my mum and dad's room, begged them to let me sleep with them. I would have screamed and shouted, no matter how much it disturbed my family and our hosts. But as I sleep, I have no idea that my life is about to change for ever. Of course I don't. Why would I?

What child, in her innocence, could possibly imagine the things that are about to happen?

What child, in her innocence, could know that grown-ups could be so evil?

What child, in her innocence, could begin to understand why?

As I sleep, he is preparing himself. He knows what is going to happen. He knows the urges that are controlling him. He knows the only thing that will satisfy them.

Worst of all, he knows where I am.

He leaves his room in the dead of night. The rest of the household asleep, he creeps along the corridor. He stops outside my door. His breath is unsteady with excitement, and so are his hands. Slowly, quietly, the door opens and he steps inside, closing the door silently behind him. For a few moments he looks down at the little girl in the bed, fast asleep. She will be awake soon, but when that happens he knows how he will keep her quiet, both for the moment and in the future.

He's got it all worked out.

I am allowed a few more seconds of blissful sleep. Of innocence and ignorance of the terrible things that can happen to a child.

But then he takes another step towards me. He bends down and pulls back the blankets. He forces himself on top of my curled-up, sleeping body.

And so it begins.

# 1
## *Through the Window*

Remembering the past is like looking through a window.

When I think back on my life, I visualise myself gazing through that window and seeing the little girl that I used to be and all the things that happened to her. It's like looking at a different person, and at times I find myself wanting to bang furiously on the glass, attract her attention and tell her the things I know now. Maybe, if someone had done that back then, everything might have turned out differently and the events that followed might not have happened.

But memories don't work like that, and no matter how much I bang on that window, the little girl remains deaf to it, and I am forced to witness every detail of my childhood as a helpless observer. I find myself wishing I could draw a curtain, turn and look in a different direction. But that is not possible.

I was born in Southend-on-Sea, the daughter of Brian and Sandra Horgan. My mum had been born in Southend in 1945, the eldest of nine children and the only girl. Despite the large number of children, hers was a loving, stable upbringing, my nan and granddad always putting their kids first. Dad was born in the same year in Croydon. Sadly his father died when he was very young, and my grandmother went on to marry the man I came to think of as my grandfather.

When he was sixteen, my father worked on the big wheel at the fairground in Southend; Mum also worked there, on one of the other fairground rides, and that is how they met. It was 1961 – the sixties were just beginning; rock and roll was at its height. Dad must have been keen, because more often than not after he had finished work, he would ride back to Croydon on his prized motorbike and change into a dapper suit, while Mum went home and dressed up in an elegant dress and stilettos. He would then drive all the way back to Southend and take her out for the evening. Brian and Sandra would go out dancing to Elvis Presley, Buddy Holly and the other sounds of the early sixties.

The sixties may have been just starting, but the sexual revolution had not yet arrived in Southend-on-Sea. As was the norm, my parents decided to get married after they had been courting for less than a year. They were both seventeen years old by that time, and their first child – my brother Sean – arrived soon after, when they were eighteen. A second son, Stuart, was born in 1965. I came along on 30 January 1969.

We were not a wealthy family, though I don't suppose we were much worse off than most working-class families in those difficult days of the early 1970s. When it became clear that the wage of a Ferris-wheel attendant was not going to be enough to support a family, Dad took a job as a long-distance lorry driver, taking loads mostly to Northern Ireland. Mum, of course, had her hands full with us, but as we lived only round the corner from my nan and granddad's in Southend, she got a lot of help.

The nature of Dad's work meant that he was often away from home for long periods of time; perhaps it was this that put a strain on my parents' marriage; perhaps they just encountered the same problems that all married couples run into. Whatever the reasons, all I know is that one day my dad didn't come home. In Mum's books, however, families were meant to stay together, so she decided to travel to Northern Ireland to track him down.

And so I was packed off to stay with my relations while Mum went about the difficult business of saving her marriage.

My relatives' resources were limited and there wasn't much room, so Sean and Stuart, being older, were sent into foster care. How they must have felt, both of them still little boys, walking into the unfamiliar house of a strange family, I can only imagine. Years later, Sean would remember being bundled into a car while his little brother was driven away in another: the image of little Stuart looking terrified as he pressed his hands against the glass of the car window before he was driven away has stayed with him. And Stuart himself told me of his overriding memory of his foster home. He had been allowed to take a toy with him, and so he chose his beloved yellow Tonka truck. A few days after he arrived at the foster home, he was quietly playing on his own with the toy when another of the children picked it up, dropped it on the floor and smashed it to pieces. Little Stuart was inconsolable, but then the child who had broken the toy told the grown-ups that Stuart himself had done it, and my brother was punished for not taking care of his things. On other occasions, one of the other children would deliberately urinate on his bed, so that Stuart would get the blame as well as the shame. I'm sure the grown-ups didn't know what was going on, and in later life Stuart recalled that they were nice people. But children can be so unkind, and he was on the receiving end of it.

Thankfully for them, the ordeal of the foster home didn't last for long. Mum and Dad sorted things out, and the family was reunited. We upped roots and moved to Larne in Northern Ireland, just north of Belfast, where my parents found a flat above a shoe shop. This was the first home that I remember.

Mum found the move to Larne extremely hard: no family to help with looking after the kids, and no friends.

Dad still had to earn a living for us, and so he was away, regularly, from Sunday night until Friday afternoon.

Our new home was dingy and run-down. The walls were high, the windows were small. We would have liked the luxury of carpet on the floor, but there was no money for that. The floorboards were ill-fitting, splintered and rough, and they had nails sticking dangerously out of them. To walk barefoot in the bedroom would be foolish; to do so in the dark would be even more so. Much better to stay under the covers, hidden from the night and whatever terrors it might contain. From the start, life there was very hard as there was little money to go around.

I was unsettled and scared of our new house – it all felt so strange and I found it difficult to sleep. One night stands out in my mind the most; I remember it like it was yesterday. My eyes shot open. I don't recall what time it was; I only remember being terrified: the usual childhood fears of monsters under the bed and shadows against the window. Something creaked, and I pulled the covers more firmly around my body.

I lay wide-eyed in the darkness, a chill running through me. I hoped the creaking sound would go away, but it didn't. If anything it got louder. At times I thought there was something in my room. I didn't want to be by myself any more, so I slipped out from under the covers and braved the cold, nail-strewn floor. As I crept towards the door, the darkness enclosed me, stuck to me. I grew more frightened. I wanted to get back to my bed, but I had lost my bearings now and didn't know which way to turn. I started groping in the darkness, fumbling. Suddenly my fingertips brushed the doorknob. As quietly as my childlike clumsiness would allow, I opened it and stepped outside.

Now that I was in the corridor however, I was paralysed with fear. It was lighter here – perhaps a lamp was on – but no more comforting for that. I sat on the floor, hugging my knees.

Too scared to go and see my mum, too scared to go back to bed, I sat there with ever more terrifying thoughts whizzing round my mind. Thoughts of ghosts and monsters – all coming to get me.

And then, just as my fear threatened to overwhelm me, he was there.

I don't know where he came from – my memory of that flat is too hazy for me to know where his bedroom was – but his sudden presence made me jump. As I did so, my bare foot scraped along the floor and snagged on an unseen nail. Instantly my skin was covered in bright scarlet blood, the colour of poster paints. I breathed in sharply from the pain, then looked to my brother for comfort.

'I'm frightened, Stu,' I said.

Stuart was only eight years old, but he had the power to make it all OK like no adult could. He sat down next to me, put his arm around my shoulder, and pulled me tightly towards him. 'Don't worry, Jayne,' he told me reassuringly. 'There's nothing to be scared of. It'll be all right in the morning. You'll see.'

'My foot hurts,' I told him. We both looked down to see the blood on my toe, and I remember that sight making me shiver. It didn't worry Stuart, though. He reached out, and pushed his thumb against the wound. 'If you press it,' he told me, his voice patient, 'it'll stop bleeding.'

I bit my lip and allowed him to make it better. Sure enough, the flow of blood soon eased, so he took off his sock, spat on it, and wrapped it round my toe as a makeshift bandage.

'Come on,' he said. 'You can sleep in my bed tonight.'

I looked at him gratefully as he led me along the corridor to his bedroom. 'I'm still scared, Stu,' I told him when I was safely in his bed.

'I told you, Jayne, there's nothing for you to worry about. You're safe. It'll be OK in the morning.' He put his arms round me as I lay there and gave me a cuddle. 'I'll look after you,' he whispered, and I knew that he would.

He stroked my hair. 'Just go to sleep, Jayne,' he said. 'Go to sleep, and I'll be here when you wake up.'

'Do you promise?' I asked him.

'Yes, Jayne,' he replied. 'I promise.'

The big, brightly coloured, crocheted blanket with

which he had covered me smelled of old things – old houses, old people. Musty. But I didn't mind, because Stuart was there with me. And so, with that smell in my nose, and the feeling of Stuart's hand stroking my hair, I finally fell asleep.

When I awoke again, it was light. True to his word, Stuart was still there, sitting on the floor. And even though he was asleep, his hand was still clasped firmly around mine. Now that it was light outside, and the sun had dispelled the shadows from that unwelcoming flat, I wasn't frightened any more.

We did not stay above the shoe shop for long. Soon we were all packed into Dad's lorry and moved into a bigger, brighter, more comfortable house in Antiville Road. Compared to our previous place it was like a palace – though in truth it was probably very ordinary – and the day we moved in I remember Sean, Stuart and myself being astonished by the size of the windows, and running around the empty rooms, shouting to make our voices echo. It was a perfect, idyllic place. There was even a large garden where Dad built us our own little farmyard, complete with real chickens.

'Are they ours, Dad?' I asked. 'To keep?'

'Course they are, Jayne,' he replied with a smile. 'And if you learn how to look after them properly, we'll get some ducks too.'

I smiled with pleasure as he explained how to look after the chickens and, true to his word, not long after that he came home one weekend, smiling excitedly, with some ducks. Soon we had hedgehogs and frogs as well. It was paradise for a little girl.

My memories are of a warm, comfortable place where I felt happy and secure. For a time when we were at Antiville Road, I started wetting the bed. Mum was brilliant, creating a little star chart just for me and rewarding me with gold stars if I woke up dry. I was so desperate for one of those little gold stars and praise from my mum that I did the very best I could not to wet the bed, and soon I didn't need that star chart any more.

While we were at Antiville Road, there was another big change: Mum fell pregnant again. I was so excited at the prospect of a new baby in the house, and used to pester my mum with questions.

'Will it be a boy or a girl, Mum?'

'We don't know yet, Jayne. We won't know until the baby's born.'

I privately hoped it would be a girl, as I already had two brothers.

'Will I be able to play with it, Mum? Will we be friends?'

'Of course you'll be friends, Jayne. It'll be your little brother or sister.'

I started playing out little fantasies about what a good big sister I would be when the baby arrived. I would help Mum in any way I could, and look after the baby whenever she was busy doing something else. And when Mandy was first born, I was so excited. It meant Dad was around, for a start, looking after us for two weeks and spoiling us rotten while Mum was in hospital.

Dad seemed so happy about the new arrival. 'You looking forward to being a big sister?' he asked me one evening while I was helping him cook dinner for the four of us who were still at home.

I nodded enthusiastically, a big grin on my face.

Dad bent down then, and gave me a cuddle. 'It's an important job, being a big sister, you know.'

'I know, Dad. I'll try my hardest.'

'Course you will, Jayne. But you've got to always remember that you're still my little girl. I don't want you feeling left out, just because everyone's excited about the new baby.'

'Ok, Dad,' I replied happily as he hugged me tighter, before we went back to cooking dinner.

Sean, Stuart and I had a happy couple of weeks with my dad, waiting for the baby to come home. We would go for long walks, holding hands; he would tell me silly jokes and pull funny faces – I felt as close to him then as I ever have done. And when Mum and Mandy finally arrived home, I got a little present – a Barbie doll of my own. She had a yellow hat and raincoat, and little wellies just like mine. The day I was given her, it was pouring with rain, and I was allowed to walk to school with my doll dressed up in her waterproofs. It was fun, I decided, having a sister.

Reality never quite lives up to a child's expectations however, and of course things were not quite the way I imagined they would be when Mandy arrived. Up until then, I had always been the baby of the family. With Mandy's arrival, things changed. I started feeling really left out. I don't know when I first managed to convince myself that Mum preferred Mandy, but as time passed that was certainly how I felt.

It's a terrible thing for a child to convince herself that her mum loves someone else more than her, but while I never resented Mandy, I felt, probably wrongly, that I was never able to do anything right in my mum's eyes once she arrived.

On one occasion, Mum was busy cleaning the house. I thought it would be a help to her if I picked Mandy up and sat with her for a while so that she could get on with her chores uninterrupted. I took her in my arms and turned round, not realising that the vacuum cleaner was in the middle of the floor behind me. I tripped up, and Mandy fell from my arms on to the floor, hitting her head. Mum was there immediately. She took one look at the situation and quite rightly I was in really bad trouble.

I opened my mouth to try to explain what had happened, but all that came out were big sobs – distress that I had hurt my sister, of course, but also distress that I had made Mum angry with me.

Things were different between me and Mum after that. I know it was me who changed, not her, and it seemed that whenever I tried to do the right thing, I messed up in her eyes. I became worried all the time – I couldn't tell anyone how I felt, not even my dad or Stuart. I didn't want to cause any trouble or seem jealous. Deep down I knew I was being silly. From my perspective, I was always to blame, and Mandy seemed to get all the attention and love.

I became known as the clumsy one in the family.

I desperately wanted my mum's approval. But the harder I tried to please her, the clumsier I became, and as time passed, I simply learned to accept that this was the way things were. I loved my mum just like I loved my dad, but I had managed to convince myself that I was second best, and I was just going to have to get used to it.

We would have been happy to stay at Antiville Road for the rest of our childhood had we been given the opportunity. But we weren't. I don't know why we had to move out of that house, but move out of it we did, to a run-down, bombed-out area. Our new home was in a road called Hope Street.

Hope Street did not live up to its name. It was old-fashioned and practically derelict. The rooms of our house were dingy and dark, and the place did not have a proper bathroom, or even a toilet. Instead, we were forced to walk in the freezing cold to a hut at the bottom of the garden. There were perhaps fifteen houses next to each other, but on the opposite side there was a wasteland and a sewer, with occasionally a train trundling past. It was one of those parts of Northern Ireland where the years of violence and sectarianism were reflected in the very streets. Rusting shells of burned-out cars littered the road, and kids from poor families used to fight in the streets. I kept away from the rough kids. I preferred to stay inside where I was a real daddy's girl.

I would always seek affection from my dad, even down to preferring it when he washed my hair. He always hated the idea of me having short hair. 'Girls should have long hair, and that's that, Jayne,' he used to tell me. Problem was, long hair meant head lice. Whenever that happened, I would always go to him.

'Dad, I've got an itchy head.'

'OK, Jayne, love – let's have a look.'

I'd sit down for him, and he would rummage through my hair looking for the telltale white flecks. And if he found them, he was always happy to deal with them.

'Go get the shampoo, Jayne,' he would tell me. I'd run

and get the bottle that we always kept, and he would carefully rub the horrid-smelling liquid on to my head, then sit with me while it did its work.

'Can we play snap while we wait, Dad?' I would always ask him. He would smile indulgently and sit playing card games to distract me from the nasty smell. And when the time came, he would get the steel nit comb and comb it gently through my hair, explaining to me what nits do and why my head was so itchy. I hated having nits, but I liked it when Dad got rid of them for me.

Bonfire night was always a big event in Ireland. The community was glad of any kind of excuse to come together and forget about the harsh reality of life – the car bombs, the political murders. And while I don't remember those dreadful things affecting my own life, I certainly remember bonfire nights.

We kids would spend weeks trawling the neighbourhood for anything that could go on top of the massive communal bonfire that would be lit on 5 November. Anything that would burn – mattresses, chopped-down trees, broken beds – was fair game. You name it, we'd put it on the pile so that this year's bonfire would be better than the last. The piles of rubbish we accumulated came together to build bonfires that were as big as a house. Dangerous, no doubt, but they attracted all the kids from our neighbourhood, and many from the surrounding areas as well.

The icing on the cake was always the guy – a stuffed straw dummy dressed in old clothes. By the time the bonfire was built, getting the guy up to the top was a tall order in more ways than one. It was dangerous, and it needed somebody fearless and tough. My brother Stuart was that person – he may not have been the older brother, but he was certainly the more reckless. It would be his job to climb up to the top of the bonfire and place the guy in its time-honoured position. He always acted like it was no big deal – indeed, he seemed to thrive on the excitement of it.

When bonfire night came, it was fabulous. We would always have managed to create a section of the bonfire especially for cooking potatoes wrapped in tinfoil in the hot embers of the fire. The grown-ups would have music playing in the houses and would congregate on the doorsteps, drinking, smoking and enjoying the warmth in the heart of the Irish winter. We kids would drink in the heady smell of wood mixed with burning rubber as though it was the finest aroma we had ever smelled, and when the time came for us to eat our luxuriously fluffy baked potatoes, we honestly felt as though life could not get better. We would sit by the fire, listening to the crackle as it burned, until we could literally no longer stay awake and we made our way, tired but happy, to our beds.

The next day, of course, life would go back to normal. Dad would be away all week, while Mum struggled to look after us on the little that we had. Frequently there would be no electricity, so we would find ourselves huddled round a little Calor gas stove, trying to get some warmth from it as we toasted scraps of bread on the end of forks. We were not the only ones – there seemed to be a lot of women in the neighbourhood who found themselves in the same position as Mum, and if one family had their electricity cut off, others would occasionally offer to help out if they could. There wasn't always a neighbour in a position to do this, however, so more often than not we found ourselves living in the cold and the gloom. We never went without food, but there was seldom much to go round. Tins of soup would get watered down so that there was enough for us all, and we seemed to be forever eating semolina as a little went a long way and it was good for filling up hungry children.

Life was not easy for my mum and dad, but they did their best with what they had.

Being so young, I found the move to Ireland not as disorientating for me as it was for Sean and Stuart. They found themselves in rough Northern Irish schools, but they had learned to speak with pronounced Estuary accents that made them stand out as different. Kids being what they are, my brothers were almost bound to have a tough time of it.

Sean got a lot of trouble from the local kids, but Stuart especially was at the receiving end of some of the most vicious bullying it's possible to imagine. I witnessed some of these encounters, and they still stick in my mind.

On one occasion Stuart was surrounded by a crowd of jeering Irish children, some of them a good deal older than he, calling him names and then laying into him with fists and feet, kicking him and scratching him, knocking him around with big planks of rough wood. At first he would just lie there foetus-like and take it, his face locked into a determined grimace as his body absorbed the awful blows from his unkind classmates and others. And of all those images in my mind, one thing jumps out at me: not once, ever, even in the midst of the most horrific beatings, did he cry. Crying just wasn't what my brother was about. I remember sometimes even being confused as to whether they were play-fighting or not, as Stuart never seemed to display any emotion; but I understand now, of course, that beatings like that are never administered in jest.

That emotion could not be bottled up indefinitely, however. Stuart could only have been ten or eleven years old when he started drinking alcohol. I suppose seeing it in the house, our parents and their friends drinking on a regular basis as well as watching all his friends do it, was bound to have some sort of effect on him at that impressionable age, and he would later tell me stories of how he would drink from the bottles of strong, sweet cider that he had seen my dad consuming. On one occasion, after a particularly vicious and brutal beating from the cruel Irish children, he took solace in a bottle and became paralytically drunk when he was supposed to be in school. He took the bottle of cider and used it to smash a line of car wind-screens, yelling, 'Irish bastards! I fucking hate you! I hate you all.' The treatment that was meted out to him clearly engendered such anger: just because he didn't cry when he was being attacked, didn't mean that it wouldn't come out in some other form.

Nobody could undergo the brutality of the beatings for long. Stuart would either be consumed by it, or rise above it. And so, soon enough, he learned how to fight back. He learned to go for the biggest of the group – once you'd felled him, the others would surely follow. He learned that he was good at it. Slowly, he began to gain respect from his peers. It was either that, or suffer the humiliation of the constant bullying and beatings for the rest of his childhood. And while Stuart's increasingly boisterous behaviour was a source of anxiety for my mum, when Dad came home for the weekends, it was a different matter. Mum would tell him what we had all been up to during the week, and Stuart would be called in front of him.

'Your mum tells me you had a fight this week.'

'Yes, Dad,' Stuart would reply.

'Did you win?'

'Yes, Dad.'

'Good for you.'

You showed them you were not scared. It was just the way Dad was and Stuart was the same.

It wasn't the same for the girls though. I always hated violence. It frightened me, even from a very early age, and I was always extremely non-confrontational. If I had a toy and a school friend wanted it, I would automatically give it up. On my first day at nursery, I was playing with a toy till and another little girl came and took it from me. I felt sad, but of course I didn't complain. I just thought that was the right thing to do to avoid an argument and to avoid people thinking worse of me.

Who knows, perhaps if I had been a little bit more like Stuart, the devastating events of the years that followed might not even have occurred.

Despite the loneliness I felt once Mandy was born, it would be wrong of me to say that my time in Larne was unhappy. I made good friends. One in particular sticks in my mind. He was called Peter, and we thought we were special because we were like Peter and Jane in the storybooks. None of us ever had the money for toys, of course, and we were forced to make up our own games in the street: chase, hide-and-seek, making mud pies, the usual pursuits of a childhood that would soon be taken from me.

I enjoyed school too. It was run by nuns, and every morning we would have an hour-long assembly, with prayers and hymns. I loved the singing and readings, not because I was particularly religious, but because they gave me a sense of peace and togetherness – something I suppose I felt I was missing. The nuns were so kind – one of them even gave me extra reading lessons – and they went out of their way to make school fun for us. I remember being in a school play and having to dress up in a shawl and lacy bonnet like someone from a Western film. While I was on the stage I looked out and saw my mum and dad in the audience. I was so happy to see them that I started sobbing – it filled me with a nameless emotion when they came to see me. And after the play, one of the nuns gave me a cuddle and told me how well I had done. I felt very special that day.

I was always closer to Stuart than to Sean – perhaps because Sean was that bit older, but also because he never seemed to be around much. And Stuart and I just seemed to have a link, a bond. On special occasions, Stuart would take me on a 'journey'. He was popular by now, thanks to his fighting, and respected. I suppose I was happy enough for some of that to rub off on me. Sometimes we would go round stripping lead from cars and wheeling it round in a pram to the scrap merchants, who would give us a few pence for what we had delivered. Typically, however, Stuart befriended the Alsatian that guarded the scrap yard, and when we'd made our sale he would scale the wall of the yard and pinch the goods back, then wheel them round and sell them all over again to the same man. I was too young to know we were doing anything wrong, and would be delighted when Stuart gave me a handful of change to buy myself some sweets, before sending me home so that he and his mates could buy a bottle of cider and half an ounce of Golden Virginia, and sit in the burned-out shells of cars opposite the house in Hope Street.

Sometimes his newly earned respect and light-fingered ways would make him popular even with the adults in the street. On one occasion I remember waking up to find that the space underneath my bed was stuffed with Fray Bentos meat pies and Mr Kipling apple pies. Stuart and a couple of mates had raided a factory and brought their spoils home with them. There were families in Hope Street – some with even less money than us – who were fed for a month on the back of Stuart's little night-time adventure, and long after that they would stop him in the street, slap him on the back and perhaps give him a couple of pence if they could afford it so that he could go and treat himself.

On another occasion, he managed to sneak me into the cinema without paying; and because he had befriended the woman who worked at the sweet counter he was even able to ply me with popcorn and fizzy drinks, without paying a penny. My brother could charm the birds out of the trees.

It was wrong of us to get up to these things, I suppose, but we were poor, and we didn't know any better. And thinking back now, it seemed like an innocent time, like the calm before the storm, though when I look back through the eyes of an adult, I realise that life in Northern Ireland during the seventies was not without its dangers. Young as I was, Mum allowed me to go out and earn a bit of money selling newspapers on the corner of the street, and so I saw at first hand the realities of life in the streets of Northern Ireland. Wherever you went you would see grim-faced soldiers in black body armour carrying enormous riot shields and heavy-looking guns. One day I was sent to buy some bread from the corner shop. Opposite this shop was a children's clothes boutique, filled with the most wonderful clothes, the like of which I would only ever dream of owning. But on this day the boutique had been destroyed. There were boulders strewn in front of it, and smoke billowing out from its shattered windows.

As a child, you have no fear – it's something you have to learn. I approached the debris of the burned-out shop with eager anticipation. If I were to pick over the rubble, it was possible that I might find myself a pair of white socks – mine always went yellow in the wash. I ran over and started picking my way through the garments, but they were singed and brown, and the smell of them stuck in my nose.

Suddenly I heard a voice yelling, 'Oi! You! Get away from there now!' I turned to see a soldier running towards me, his face a picture of angry concern.

I had no idea what I was doing wrong, and the blood in my veins turned to ice as I ran as fast as I could towards home, the heavily armed soldier chasing after me. I burst through the front door to find Stuart there waiting for me.

'Stuart,' I cried. 'Stuart, there's a man chasing me. I think he's going to kill me.'

'Don't worry,' Stuart said, but I couldn't be calmed down as I hid in the corner of the room, trembling.

'Mum's going to be cross,' I whimpered, my Irish accent by now as thick as anyone's. 'I was supposed to be getting some bread.'

Stuart smiled at me, then took the money and ran off to buy the bread himself. 'Whatever you do,' he said when he got back, 'don't tell Mum.'

But being secretive was not in my nature, and I found it difficult to keep my adventures to myself; so later that day I told my mum about the shop that used to be there but wasn't any more.

'Yeah,' Mum replied, almost nonchalantly. 'A bomb went off last night.'

'What's a bomb, Mum?'

'Don't worry about it, Jayne. Stop asking questions.'

I knew it was all the response I was going to get, but

from that day on it was as if my eyes had been opened to the world around me. It became commonplace to see police in armoured tanks raiding a building. I became aware of the heightened security; I became aware of the police presence; I became aware of the fact that everyone – even children – was thoroughly searched every time we went into a department store. It became normal to me to have to hand over my prized little pink bag to an armed soldier wherever I went. I asked my mum why they always did this. 'Do they want to take our sweets or something?'

'No, Jayne. They don't want to take your sweets.' She sat me down beside her. 'What you have to remember is that there's a lot of bad people in the world, and they do bad things. The soldiers just want to make sure that they don't do bad things to us.'

I listened, but said nothing. Bad things to us? What could she mean? Who would want to do bad things to me?

Soon though, the soldiers were to disappear from our lives. But in any case, all the soldiers in the world wouldn't have been able to stop what happened next . . .

## 2

# Farewell to Hope Street

Once or twice a year, the family would be packed on to a ship and we would make the journey back to the mainland to visit my nan and granddad and other family in Southend. It was something we all looked forward to. A holiday.

I was eight years old when the six of us embarked upon one of these trips. I don't remember ever being told that in fact this was more than a visit, that we had moved back to the mainland for good; nor did I twig that this was the case. Perhaps it was because we stayed with a number of different families – various friends and relations of my parents – and so it did seem like a holiday to begin with. More likely, it was simply the case that if you don't tell young children things, they won't necessarily work them out for themselves. Had I been a little older, or a little more intuitive, perhaps I would have read the signs a bit better. The bombs in our area had been going off with increased frequency: sometimes I would hear the explosions as I was lying in bed at night; more often, I overheard the serious, semi-whispered discussions of the grown-ups. The police and army presence was visibly on the increase. And then, one day, I remember my mum and dad coming home in a dreadful panic; for some reason, Stuart hid Mandy and myself under a stereo unit and we stayed there, frightened, while we listened to the shouts of an angry stranger on the other side of the door. What was happening, I have no idea, but we moved soon after that.

At first I thought that the holiday was going on a bit longer than the others. Then I started asking my mum questions. 'We've been on holiday for a long time, Mum. When are we going home?'

'Not for a little while yet,' she would reply evasively, no doubt not wanting the stress of a tearful daughter on her hands.

'What about my school work?' I would ask. Even when I started attending a local school I don't think I quite realised that we weren't going back to Northern Ireland at all.

What I did know, however, was that I missed home. I missed my friends. I even missed my old school. It was a gentle place, despite being nestled in the heart of such a violent area, run by nuns who were always kind and considerate and keen to make us part of a community. My new school was the very opposite: impersonal, unfriendly and huge. The teachers had to deal with far larger groups of children than those sweet nuns back in Larne, so there was no way they could give us the same kind of attention. To make things worse, I was different: not only was I the new girl, I had a striking Irish accent, which made me stand out; and I was disorientated and out of place. I hated it, and didn't understand why we couldn't go back to the friends and the life I had left behind me in Ireland. I was too confused and timid to ask my parents why everything was so different, and so I suffered in silence as we moved from lodging to lodging, relying on the kindness of friends and distant family we barely knew, wondering what was going on and trying to make sense of it all.

After a few weeks, however, there was one small cause for excitement. A street party was just around the corner, and everyone was preparing for it. My mum and dad were still looking for a place to live, so by this time we were staying temporarily in Wales with distant relatives I'd never heard of. In truth I can remember very little about them, with the exception of one person: he was also staying with the family and was a distant relative of mine, from a different branch of the family from the one we were staying with, though too distant for me to be able to work out the precise relationship even now. He was much older than I – a man – and popular with my parents and the other grown-ups; but I remember feeling uncomfortable in his presence the first time I met him. There was something about him: he seemed detached, different – just weird. He was not like anybody I had known in Ireland, and I didn't like the way he looked at me. I would catch him staring, just staring at me. When I caught his eye, he would smirk and wink at me, as if I knew what he was thinking. It made me blush and turn away. I didn't like it, or know why he was singling me out when there were others around. I tried just to be quiet and keep out of his way.

He had small, sharp eyes of a piercing green; his hair was a tousled mop of ginger and his skin was pink and blotchy where he shaved. He dressed neatly – a bit too neatly – with his T-shirts always tucked immaculately into his jeans and his shoes always shiny and perfectly tied. He always smelled of strong aftershave. His name was Graham. When we first met, he shook my hand and said, 'Hello, J-J.' I cringed at the affectionate name – it seemed horribly inappropriate and I didn't want him to call me that. Nobody called me that – why should he?

'Hello,' I replied, pulling my hand quickly away. After that first meeting I did my best to keep out of his way, but no matter how hard I tried he always seemed to be there, in every room I was sitting in, lurking around whatever corner.

The street party was to be a fabulous occasion, and I was really excited. Bunting was being draped across the rooftops, and trestle tables were to extend the length of the road, which would be shut off to cars so that it could be given over to the more important purpose of merrymaking. The children would be allowed to stay up late, and there would be lots of nice food and fizzy drinks for us. Stuart and Sean talked excitedly about how much fun it was going to be, and I found myself getting caught up in their enthusiasm as I followed them around, wanting to be a part of everything.

It wasn't only the children who were excited – the grown-ups too were looking forward to this party. Untold numbers of barrels of beer and bottles of wine were ordered in, and I remember having the instinct that this would be different from anything I had witnessed back in Ireland. Even at my young age I had picked up on the sense of excitement in the air. And so, even though I longed to be back in Ireland with my friends, there was at least something to look forward to in the days ahead. Something to take my mind off how lonely I felt.

The children attending the street party were to wear fancy-dress costumes. It was blistering hot on the day – a couple of days before the party – that we had our costumes made. The grown-ups made a real fuss of us, sewing on bright sequins and pearly buttons so that we felt special. Of course, the novelty soon wore off and, rather than be stuck indoors, we wanted to be outside playing; but it was a happy day none the less, and I went to bed tired yet full of excitement for the party.

The house where we were staying was big – big enough

for us all to fit in. Our hosts had assigned me a little boxroom, and I was quite comfortable there. Mum and Dad were in a big double room next door, and they had made a little bed for Mandy in the bottom drawer of a chest of drawers. My pillow was soft, my blanket was warm, and the day had been fun; but even so it took me a while to go to sleep that night. As always, once darkness descended my thoughts became more active. I found myself wishing that I could have been sharing the fun with my friends back home rather than being stuck here in Wales, and I started to feel sad and homesick. Eventually, however, I nodded off. My dreams that night were filled with images of bunting, fancy-dress costumes and party food. Happy dreams.

I don't know what time it was when I awoke, but it was pitch-black in my bedroom. I was warm and drowsy, but even in my sleepy state I could instantly tell that something was not right.

I felt pain.

There was someone in my bed with me.

Sleep fell away.

I could tell it was Graham who was with me beneath the blanket – I could smell him, that heavy aftershave he always wore that clung to the walls when he left a room, so strong it felt suffocating in my throat, as if I was being strangled. I recognised his heavy breathing. But I had no idea what he was doing to me. Why would I? I was eight years old. All I knew was that he was lying on top of me, his skin pressed against my nightie. And he was doing something that really, really hurt. I didn't know what sex was; I didn't know that that was what grown-ups did. Whatever it was that was happening was so far beyond the realms of my experience and knowledge that I didn't even know whether this was something that he should be doing or not.

The pain was like something I had never experienced. All small children get tummy aches, and I was no exception, but what I was feeling now was so much more than that. All encompassing. All consuming. My whole belly was in agony, all the way up to my chest, and the more he carried on doing whatever it was he was doing, the more it hurt – a horrible, burning, piercing sensation, as though someone had inserted a red-hot poker into me and was wiggling it around with no thought for the trauma it was causing me.

The longer he continued, the more my vision grew accustomed to the darkness; I could see his eyes now, and his features. His face was contorted into a grimace, and his flat eyes refused to look at me – not that I wanted them to. I screwed up my own eyes, and waited for it to be over. But at one stage I did open them, and I caught his glance. I did not understand the emotion that I saw in his face, but the more I looked at him the more I saw it change into fear – fear, I suppose, that he would be caught doing this. Whether or not he had expected me to remain asleep while he satisfied his desires I don't know, but that was the impression I had.

How long it lasted I couldn't say; not as long, probably, as the eternity that it seems to be in my memory. All the while, a little voice inside my head was crying out, shrieking for my mummy, shrieking to be taken back to Ireland where horrible things like this didn't happen. At one stage I opened my mouth to cry out, but there was no sound there. Just emptiness and silence. I did not so much as whisper.

And then it was all over.

As he painfully withdrew and heaved his heavy body off mine, the discomfort I had been feeling was suddenly rushed by a river of other emotions. Confusion, of course, but also horror – a terrible, all-pervading horror that made me tremble weakly. I didn't realise I had just been raped – rape wasn't even a word I knew – and I didn't realise that what I should really have done was run to safety and make as much noise as possible. That wasn't in my nature, anyway.

Instead I froze. It seemed that I lay there for hours – in truth it was probably only a few minutes – with Graham's hand over my mouth. I could feel the clammy moistness on his palm as he pressed hard against my face, starving me of oxygen. I felt trickles of sweat running down my cheek as I struggled for breath, and the only thing that made me believe I might survive this were the little bubbles of air escaping from my nose as I cried desperately and in repressed silence.

Then I heard his voice. He was whispering softly and cruelly into my ear: 'I swear to God, J-J,' he told me, 'if you tell anyone, I'll kill you.'

There was a pause, and then he repeated, 'I'll kill you, J-J. Mention one word of this to anyone, and I'll kill you.'

He repeated himself several times, never raising his voice; but each time he spoke, the words rang in my ears like church bells and I could sense a genuine evil about him.

'Do you understand, Jayne?'

I nodded. There was no doubt in my young mind that he meant exactly what he said. He sounded sure of himself. Confident. He could get away with it, and no one would ever know.

'I'm going to move my hand away now,' he said. 'When I do that, you had better not say a word, or you're fucking dead and that's a promise.' He paused for a moment, then moved his hand from my face; instantly, however, as though to reiterate what he had just said, he fiercely grabbed my wrist, then bent my arm behind my back until I was teetering on the brink of agony. 'You'll die,' he repeated. 'You'll fucking die if you say a word of this to anyone.'

No one had ever used such language to me before, and the swearing itself would have been enough to make me crumble; as it was, I felt literally as if the life was being frightened out of me.

'I'm getting out of bed now,' he said. 'But I'm staying here, in your room. Don't even think of getting up to tell anyone.'

I answered only with terrified silence as he climbed out of bed and lay on the floor.

I curled up into a little ball, hedgehog-like, beneath my covers. I tried to stop myself crying because I knew it would make him angry, but that was impossible: huge racking sobs welled up in my chest, and I pulled my pillow hard into my face to muffle the sound of choking tears.

Time passed. He didn't say a word, but I could sense his presence there, silent and threatening. I longed to get out of the room, and I found myself wondering if he had fallen asleep. As if in answer to my unspoken question, I heard him snoring. It was a relief, but I was still too frightened to make any sudden actions. And so I made tiny, tiny movements towards the edge of the bed. Some of those movements were so small as barely to be movements at all, and to my mind it took an age for me even to get to the edge of the bed. Every time I shifted, the quiet whisper of my body against the bedclothes sounded like a roar. If I wasn't careful, I knew I would wake him. My skin was clammy from the fear of what he would do to me if he thought I was trying to get away, and yet I knew that was what I had to do. I could not bear to stay another moment in the same room as him.

Suddenly I couldn't stand it any longer. I jumped out of bed, and to my horror he shot up. His snores had been nothing but acting. 'Stay where you are,' he hissed, as his arms flailed around, trying to grab me. What gave me the courage to do anything other than stand statue-still I can't say, but I was halfway to the door by now and knew that I could just get away without him catching me. Terrified, I slipped outside. Surely he wouldn't follow me here; surely he wouldn't risk being caught with me on the landing in the small hours of the morning.

The house was silent as, shivering from cold and fear, I groped my way along the corridor. I felt as though I was in a dream, desperate to run away but seemingly taking for ever to reach my destination, knowing that a monster was snapping at my heels. Suddenly I heard his voice behind me: 'That's it,' he spat. 'You're dead, you fucking bitch. Get back here now.' I froze. And as I did, the pain in my stomach twisted like a knife wound. That alone allowed me to overcome my fear and continue my groping search for my parents' room. Eventually my shaking hands happened upon the door and I walked inside.

They were asleep, of course. The whole house was asleep. For a moment I stood there, alone in the darkness, and wondered whether I should wake my mum up, and what I should say if I did. As frightened as I was of what was awaiting me outside the room, I was also scared of disturbing my mother. What would she say if I told her? Would she think I had been bad? Should I tell her what had happened? In reality it was an impossible decision for me to make, because I didn't *know* what had happened. I only knew it wasn't right, that I was in so much pain and I needed someone to help me.

Timidly I stepped forward, and as I did, I felt something dripping down between my legs.

Alarmed, I put my fingers to it. It was warm and sticky. Blood.

That was it. I didn't know where the blood was coming from, or why it was coming. But I knew what it meant. I knew I was dying.

'Mum,' I whispered.

She didn't stir, so I kneeled down beside her, tapped her tentatively on the arm and whispered again a little more loudly – though not so loudly as to risk making myself heard in the next-door bedroom. 'Mum. *Can you wake up a minute?*'

'What is it, Jayne?' Mum's voice was drowsy, as Dad's loud snores filled the room.

I faltered. Now I was here, I couldn't find the words to describe what had just happened: I didn't know what his genitals were called; I didn't know what he had been doing.

'I've got a bellyache, Mum.' It was the only way I could think of saying it.

There was a pause, and I waited expectantly for my mum to say something, to hold me in her arms – somehow to understand. But how *could* she understand? I hadn't told her anything.

'Jayne,' she murmured, 'it's the middle of the night. You're going to wake everyone up. Go to bed and try and go to sleep.' She rolled over under the comfort of her blankets and nudged Dad in an attempt to turn him over and stop his snoring.

A sickness rose in my throat. I was not the type of girl to fight my corner; I was more likely to shrink away, and that was what I did.

I stood still, her words filling me with despair. I felt as if all the wind had been punched out of me. My lower lip trembled, and in that moment I felt like the loneliest, most lost little girl in the whole world.

'Sorry, Mum,' I said quietly. And then, mutely, I turned and made for the door. From the measured sounds of my mum's heavy breathing, I could tell that she was already asleep.

I felt scared to leave the room, but I knew I couldn't stay there for fear of waking Mum and Dad up. Cautiously I stepped outside. To my momentary relief, Graham wasn't in the corridor, so I crept quietly to the bathroom and locked the door behind me. Once inside, I lay down on the cold floor and dissolved into uncontrollable tears. I was in shock – my whole body was shaking and my skin felt icy. And, of course, the pain in my belly refused to go away. Despite being so cold, I felt the sweat pouring off me, and then I remembered the blood between my legs. I looked, and was horrified by the way it had smeared and dried on my skin. I was fearful enough of blood as it was, but this was different from a scraped knee in the playground, and I started to panic. I didn't understand where it had come from, or why it was there; but I was ashamed of it nevertheless. I've got to wipe this blood away, I thought to myself. I've got to be a good girl and wipe it away, otherwise I'll get everyone in trouble.

I truly believed at that point that if anyone saw me in this state I would be told off for being bad and causing a scene. I didn't want to disappoint my parents. I didn't want to let anyone down.

Still crying and trembling, I ran the tap, wetted some tissue and wiped between my legs, cleaning myself up and doing my best not to leave any trace of myself in the bathroom. I worked slowly, but I knew that I could not stay in there all night. I knew that at some stage I would have to return to the bedroom to face the monster that was waiting for me there. My mind was a riot of confusion, but of all the complicated, childish emotions that ran through my head, one was the most dominant: I thought I had seen my mum and dad for the last time. I was going to walk back into the bedroom and he would do what he said he was going to do. He was going to kill me. I didn't know how he would do it, but I knew that somehow he would.

I stood in that bathroom, scared and alone, and prepared myself for death.

My eight-year-old consciousness didn't know what happened when you died. I knew that you got buried, but not that you were put in a box first, or that you had no sensation or feelings. I imagined myself in a hole in the cold ground, the earth pressing against my lifeless body and the worms wriggling over me and boring into my skin. I would be able to do nothing, just lie there, knowing that I would never see my parents again. Never touch them. Never feel them close.

As though in a dream, I unlocked the bathroom door and numbly walked back into my bedroom.

The very minute I entered, he was upon me. He grabbed hold of my mouth and I felt his nails hard against my skin as he dug his fingers deep into the flesh of my cheeks. 'You little fucking bitch,' he hissed.

I held my breath and waited for it to happen.

He squeezed harder; I looked at him, wide-eyed, all my strength sapped from my body through fear. I suppose he must have realised from my demeanour that I hadn't told anybody about what happened, and he must have felt that his threats towards me had worked. If so, he was right.

'I'm going to let you off this time,' he said, 'but I'm telling you – try anything like that again and I *will* kill you.'

I nodded, hoping that it would stop him from hurting me.

'It's not like anyone's going to believe you anyway, you lying little bitch.'

He was right. Who was going to believe me, an eight-year-old girl, over him? I had been stupid to imagine that anyone would believe such things had happened.

He let go of me with a contemptuous flick of his hand, and in that moment I remember feeling not frightened that it was all going to happen again, but overcome with relief that I was still alive. He wasn't going to kill me. Not today. I wasn't going to be buried. I wasn't going to feel the soil against my face. I was going to see my mum and dad again. I rushed towards my bed, huddling down under my covers and cuddling my pillow, tears of relief soaking the linen of my bedclothes.

We were not a religious family. Despite having lived in the heart of sectarian Northern Ireland, where it was a matter of social and political standing whether you were Protestant or Catholic, we never went to church regularly. Political divides were not for children, and I understood them no better than anyone else my age. My only real knowledge of religion came from the nuns at school back in Larne and that, to be honest, was sketchy at the best. Certainly, I had never prayed at night. All that was about to change. That night I prayed with all my might. I did not complain to the God I barely knew; instead I thanked Him. I thanked Him for not letting me die; I thanked Him for the fact that I would see my family again in the morning and not be consigned to a cold grave by the man I knew would kill me just like he'd said he would; and when I had done thanking Him, I begged Him to keep me safe from that moment on.

Hidden under the flimsy protection of my blanket, I don't know when it was that my abuser left the room; I simply continued offering up my silent, tear-strewn prayers until the blackness of a troubled sleep finally overcame me.

When I woke up the following morning in that house in Wales, for a split second I thought I was back in Larne. But soon the horrible reality of the previous night's events came crashing in on me. Instantly I felt dirty, demoralised and confused.

I lay there for a moment, trying to summon the courage to start the day. I didn't want to get up, didn't want to face anybody – especially him. But I wouldn't be allowed to stay in bed all day, so eventually and reluctantly, I clambered weakly out. As I moved, I felt a pain in my abdomen, so I went straight to the bathroom and locked myself in. Sitting on the toilet, I noticed small bruises between my legs, each one about the size of my thumbprint. It wasn't the bruises that hurt, however; it was my belly. Still aching from the previous night, it felt as if there were sharp, stabbing pains running through it. Worse even than that, however, was the uneasy sensation that everything was wrong. That something had happened in my life that meant that nothing would ever be the same again.

But at least the bleeding had stopped.

For the second time in only a few hours, I kneeled down on the floor of that bathroom and wept. I ached to go home, back to Ireland and back to my friends, away from this monster who seemed to have appeared in my life from nowhere. I cried and cried, until finally the tears wouldn't come any more. But I couldn't stay in there for ever – there were a lot of people in the house, and sooner or later someone would be knocking on the door wanting to use the bathroom. I had to get myself together and go down to face him. To face them all. I feared that just by looking at me they would know I was dirty and bad, but I didn't have any choice. I washed my face and stepped outside.

I could hear their laughter echoing from the kitchen as I walked down the stairs. They were happy and joking, and the noises they were making were a stark contrast to the agony I was feeling inside. I appeared in the doorway of the kitchen to see Mum sitting at the table being handed a cup of tea by Graham. Everyone else was there – Stuart, Sean and the family with whom we were staying. Everyone except Dad, I think, who must have gone out to work.

'Morning, Jayne,' Mum said brightly.

I didn't answer.

Graham turned to me. 'Hello, J-J,' he said, a wolfish smile spreading over his face. 'Do you want some cereal?'

Just hearing his voice made me nauseous and seemed somehow to compound the pain in my stomach. 'Not from you,' I told him. 'I hate you. I don't want anything from you.'

Silence fell on the room as everybody turned to look at me. I heard the clinking of somebody's spoon against a breakfast bowl.

'*Jayne,*' my mum whispered, shocked at what I had just said. 'What's happened to your manners?'

I hung my head and looked at the floor. I knew there was no way I could possibly tell anyone what had really happened, so this was my only defiant way of rebelling. 'I don't want any breakfast from him,' I repeated, my voice surly. 'I hate him.'

'I'm only trying to be nice,' Graham said in a whinging kind of voice.

'You're acting,' my mum told me, understandably

furious with my unexplained outburst, 'like a spoiled little girl.' Her chair scraped back as she stood up to come to deal with me.

As she did so, Graham intervened. 'Don't worry about it,' he said nonchalantly. 'She doesn't mean it, do you, J-J? She's probably just missing home.'

Mum stopped in her tracks, looked at Graham, looked at me, and then sat down again. 'You're very lucky, my girl,' she said, 'that Graham is sticking up for you. Now sit down and behave.'

I didn't know what to say. I looked at Graham with all the loathing I could muster, but of course it meant nothing to anyone else. Mum didn't know any different – she was just reacting to what she heard, and she continued to reprimand me as I took my seat at the table and tried to eat an unwanted breakfast. For the second time since the rape, I felt the unmistakable cold touch of loneliness.

But I wasn't alone. As the tellings-off for my outburst continued, one person came to my defence. I don't think Stuart had taken a great liking to Graham from the outset, and he knew that behaviour such as I had just displayed was not in character for me.

'Oh, leave her alone,' he snapped. 'She probably *is* missing home. What's wrong with that?'

And as soon as he spoke, everything seemed slightly different. It was still awful, of course; I still hurt in my tummy and in my heart; I still had to suffer the presence in the room of the person who only a few hours previously had brutally ripped my childhood from me; I still feared that he would kill me if I so much as hinted what had happened; I still desperately wanted to escape, to return home to Ireland.

But in Stuart I had the one thing that I thought had been denied me – the one thing that maybe would help me get through this.

I had a friend.

# 3
## Almost Human

That awful breakfast seemed to last for ever. My outburst had made everyone feel uncomfortable, and the rest of the meal had been spent in awkward silence.

When everyone had finally finished, Stuart announced, 'I'm taking Jayne out for a walk,' and giving me a nod he scraped his chair back and left the room. I followed.

'Take no notice of them, Jayne,' Stuart told me. I nodded.

We wandered together out of the house, side by side, and for the longest time after that we said nothing to each other. We didn't have to – there was something unspoken between my brother and me that meant sometimes there was no need for words. It was at that moment that, despite my youth, a mature thought crystallised in my mind. With so many people, I realised, love was conditional: it was only given on the proviso that it was reciprocated in some way. But not with Stuart. The brotherly love I received from him was unconditional. He didn't care that I had been rude; he didn't care that I had been quiet and surly. I knew even then how it must have looked to everyone – that I was a horrible little child, spoiled and unpleasant because I wanted to go back home. As far as Stuart was concerned, though, I was his sister and that was that. He'd stick by me through anything.

We walked aimlessly down the street; as we did so, I barely noticed all the preparations that were going on for the party the following day – my mind was somewhere else as I kept reliving the events of the night before. I remembered the way Graham's weight kept pressing against me; the hotness of his breath on my skin; the violation of my body, the pain and the horror. All the while, Stuart stayed by my side, allowing me my silence.

I don't know how long we had been walking before we found ourselves sitting together on a wall. The morning sun was warm on our faces, and as we sat there I became invigorated with the confidence of the daytime. I smiled nervously at Stuart; he smiled back, and I suddenly felt the stirrings of courage deep inside. Maybe I should tell my brother. He, of all people, would believe me, wouldn't he? He was my best friend; we told each other everything, shared all our thoughts.

'I've got a bad bellyache, Stu,' I told him quietly, my eyes fixed firmly on the ground; and for every word that came out of my mouth, a thousand other words echoed in my brain.

For a minute he didn't reply. I sat perfectly still, but inside my head a little voice was screaming at me. 'Tell him,' it said. *'Just tell him*. Tell him what he did. Tell him he touched you, that he hurt you.' I was so close to obeying that silent instinct; but not close enough. How could I word it? What could I say? I still didn't know how to explain what had happened, and I worried that if I said anything it would make people angry with me.

'What d'you eat last night?' he asked me.

I felt a chill run through me as I realised I wasn't brave enough to tell him the truth. Instead, I told him in a level voice what I'd had for dinner the previous night.

'It's probably just a tummy bug, Jayne,' he told me. 'It'll be better soon.'

I nodded. 'Probably,' I said, and together we walked back to the house.

I moped around all day, trying to stay out of everyone's way. If a grown-up saw me, they would tell me off for being miserable, or try to cajole a good mood out of me, but without success. I didn't smile, I didn't laugh. I lost count of the times I saw people mouth to each other, 'She's missing home.' I didn't let on that I'd seen, and I didn't contradict them – I didn't want to get into more trouble, I couldn't bear that to happen.

That day I learned the meaning of dread. It was gloriously hot and sunny, the perfect childhood summer's day. But I knew that every passing second meant that we were a second closer to nightfall. I had never liked the night-times, but now they contained a new horror. All afternoon the weight of apprehension grew heavier and heavier as time inevitably passed. I knew last night was only the beginning of horrible times for me. I knew from the way he had sworn and hissed at me after he had done those terrible things; I knew from the way it had come out of nowhere. I hated it here and I hated Graham and what he had done to me.

The awful moment when the sun sank in the sky and dusk fell seemed to be upon me before I knew it.

'Jayne! Bedtime!'

A wave of nausea crashed over me, the horrific sickness of pure fear. As I said good night to the grown-ups, and then to Stuart and Sean, Graham was there, but he didn't look at me. He doesn't need to, I told myself. Everything had changed for ever. After last night I knew he would be seeing me soon enough.

I climbed the stairs, my feet feeling as heavy as my heart, and walked into my bedroom to get ready for bed. I undressed, got into my nightie and waited for Mum to come up and say good night.

After a few minutes she walked into my room. I could tell from the look on her face that I was going to be told off. 'You were very rude to Graham this morning, Jayne.'

My lip wobbled as I tried to hold back the tears.

'I don't want to hear you talking to anyone like that again, do you understand? We're guests in this house.'

I wanted to tell her, so much. But I couldn't. 'Sorry, Mum,' was all I managed, and she nodded, a cross look still on her face. But she did at least come and kiss me on the forehead and wish me sweet dreams. As she bent over me, I wrapped my arms tightly around her neck and clung on, not wanting her to leave but unable to express myself in any other way. For a little while – perhaps a minute – she remained hunched over me, allowing the hug to continue. Soon, though, I felt her hands trying to unwind my arms from her neck. I clung tighter, but as I did I heard a small huff of impatience from my mum.

'Come on, Jayne,' she said. 'It's time to go to sleep now.' She firmly unwrapped my arms, then switched off the light, left and closed the door quietly behind her.

I lay there in the darkness for a few moments. Once I had heard her footsteps fade away and I could be sure there was no movement outside my room, I slipped out of bed and pulled my clothes back on, my childlike logic suggesting to me that if there were more layers between him and my body, it would make it more difficult for him to repeat what he had done to me last night. Then I climbed back into bed, hugged the covers tightly around myself, and waited. There was no chance of falling asleep quickly – instead I lay in the darkness, wide-eyed and anxious. After a few hours I heard the sounds of the rest of the household going to bed. I closed my eyes and prayed to God to keep me safe.

I waited in the darkness and the silence. I cried and cried, and when the tears had run dry I lay still. Then I cried some more.

I don't know what time it was that sleep finally released me from the agony of waiting, but it was certainly very late. When I awoke again, it was with a start. I sat up straight and looked around.

Light was flooding in through the windows. Morning had arrived.

I looked down at myself to see that I was fully clothed, and for a moment I couldn't work out why.

Then I remembered, and the false walls of hope came crashing down again. He had left me alone for one night; but instinctively I knew that my reprieve would not be permanent.

It was now the day of the street party, and for all the other children the excitement had reached fever pitch. Last-minute adjustments were being made to everyone's outfits and everyone was so excited.

Everyone, that is, except me.

Throughout the day I was told off for being miserable and moody. 'What are you trying to do?' Mum kept asking me. 'Spoil the day for everyone?' It must have seemed to her that was exactly what I was doing, and I knew I was being difficult but I was so sad and scared. And to make matters worse, *he* always seemed to be around, joking with the grown-ups as he helped out with the preparation of all the party foods. When I refused to do as I was told, he said, 'Come on, Jayne. Be a good girl and go out and play in the garden like your mum says.' I gave him a dirty look as frustration and injustice welled up in me once more, then left the room.

A little bit later, Mum wanted me to try on my outfit again. 'I don't want to,' I snapped. 'I'm not going to the party.'

Reaching breaking point, Mum pulled me to one side. 'You had better stop this nonsense, Jayne,' she told me, 'otherwise you're going to get a smack.'

I looked at her as I tried to hold back the tears. 'All right,' I said stroppily. 'I will go to the stupid party.'

I was too young, I suppose, to understand that my attitude was only making things worse, but at least I then had the sense to keep myself to myself as I waited for the party to start. If I had known how to run away – or even known what running away *was* – that's what I'd have done. I'd have left Wales there and then, gone straight back to Ireland and my friends. I loved my family, but at that moment in time I wouldn't have missed them – not Mum, not Dad, not Sean, not Mandy. The only person I'd have missed would have been Stuart. But I was too little, or too innocent, to know that you *could* run away. I'd never heard of anyone doing it, so the idea never entered my mind. Instead, I felt as though I was trapped by my tormentor, unable to escape.

The street party started, and even though I had been around the preparations for the past few days, I was still astonished by the scale of it. The whole road was full of people enjoying themselves, the happy buzz of loud voices talking in colourful Welsh accents was all around. It was big and bright, friendly and boisterous. Despite myself, I found that I wanted suddenly to become involved. I guess that what was unfolding before my eyes was the exact opposite of what I was feeling inside, and perhaps I felt that by joining in I could forget all the horrible things that had happened, if only for a little while. But I loitered on the edge of the party, a straggle-haired little Irish kid with few friends in that strange town, wanting to take part, but not knowing how.

Until, that is, Stuart took me under his wing. His charm had already endeared him to a crowd of the local kids, and it wasn't long into the proceedings that he grabbed my hand and dragged me over to be introduced. 'This is my sister Jayne,' he announced. 'You've all got to look out for her, OK?'

His adoring new friends – many of them girls – nodded,

and for the rest of the day I was never alone. When the music played I had people to dance with, when there were games I had people to play them with. The whole thing was such an eye-opener for me. After the poverty of Larne, I was surrounded by relatively well-off children. Not rich, certainly, but they had board games and toys – not makeshift things that they'd had to construct themselves, but real toys – and they knew games, like musical chairs, that I had never even heard of. The time passed, and I found that, despite my earlier attitude, I was enjoying myself. I even occasionally forgot my ordeal of two nights earlier.

The party was in full swing when Stuart approached me and took me to one side. 'You OK?' he asked.

I nodded with what I suppose was a sad kind of smile. 'Yeah.'

'It's all right here, isn't it?'

I looked around. Everyone seemed happy, and in a way I suppose he was right. There were no more petrol bombs going off around us; the familiar sight of burned-out cars in every street were now just a memory; the smell of burning fires had been replaced with a cleaner, sweeter atmosphere; flowers bloomed, trees were everywhere, the houses were bright and clean and cheerful.

It would be beyond my skill to explain to my brother why it was that every ounce of my being longed to be back in scruffy, dirty, poor, dangerous Ireland, so I kept quiet.

'Don't take any notice of Mum,' he continued. 'She doesn't mean to keep telling you off. She's worried, that's all.'

I nodded, then took Stuart's hand and went back to join the party, where I knew I could put my troubles from my mind.

For a little while, I forgot that I was that dirty little girl. For a little while.

It was late by the time the party finished, and I was tired. Mercifully, I fell asleep the moment my head hit the pillow and slept soundly until the morning sun streamed through the window the following day. As soon as I awoke, however, my little hands felt my body. Quite what I was feeling for I don't know – just some indication of whether anything untoward had happened in the middle of the night. But all was well. For the second night in a row I had remained untouched, and there was a sense of relief about that. But the enjoyment I had experienced the day before had dissipated, and once more I found myself feeling lonely and homesick. That day I remember sitting outside with Stuart and being suddenly overcome with tears.

'What's wrong, Jayne?' He put his arm round me. 'Why are you so upset?'

'I really want to go back home, Stu,' I whispered. 'I don't

like it here. I'm sad.' Yet again I failed to tell him the real reason for my sorrow.

He squeezed me a little tighter. 'You know we're not *going* back home, don't you?'

As I heard those words, it was as though I was receiving blows to the stomach. I suppose I must have suspected as much, but to hear the truth from Stuart's mouth was almost more than I could bear.

'But I don't want to stay here, Stu,' I said in a small voice. 'I want to go home.' I looked appealingly at him. '*You* take me home,' I begged. 'We can go back together, just us two.'

'No, Jayne,' he said kindly. 'We can't do that, it's not allowed.'

I didn't understand why not, so I buried my face in my hands and cried some more while my brother did his best to comfort me.

It took a long time for me to get used to the idea of somewhere other than Ireland being home, and the fact that I had been abused in this new land only made it harder. For days and then weeks after the first time it happened, the horror of that night would be my first thought when I woke in the morning and my last thought as I cried myself to sleep at night. But as time passed, and my nights remained uninterrupted, I started to think that maybe it had been a one-off. Even the emotional wounds Graham had inflicted started to heal, and I would approach bedtime with less apprehension. Less fear. Sometimes I even went to sleep without crying.

But even then, I think I knew that something was not right. I would watch Graham during the day in his dealings with the others in the house. He would be so nice to everyone, so helpful, and they all appeared to lap it up. I was the only one who knew the truth about him, and I couldn't understand why everyone was so gullible. Couldn't they see what he was really like? Couldn't they see the truth? Of course, I now realise that this was all part of his plan – nobody had any reason to suspect him of being anything other than the friendly guy he presented himself to be – but at the time it just made me feel more confused. And the more he ingratiated himself with everybody else, the more difficult it became for me to say anything. Who would ever believe *me* over *him*?

We were not able to stay in that house forever. The time came, after several weeks, when Mum and Dad secured us a place of our own, across the border in England. When I learned that we were to move out of that house – away from Graham and everything that he had done – I was overcome with relief, as though a heavy weight had been lifted from my shoulders. Our own house, away from him. It was not quite the same as going back to Ireland, but at least I would be free from my abuser and his insidious ways. At least I would have escaped and would only have to deal with the memory of what he had done to me, not with the horrific threat that it might happen again.

Or so I thought.

Our new home was a large flat with an extension outside that my parents turned into another bedroom. Dad was still driving lorries at the time, but as we children were now older, Mum also took a job working in a pub. Stuart and Sean were of an age when they were often out playing with their friends, and so they were not always willing to look after my little sister Mandy and myself. And so, Mum had to find someone suitable to babysit on the nights when she was working in the pub.

Someone she knew.

Someone she trusted.

Someone responsible.

How it was that Graham ended up looking after us whenever my parents worked is an astonishment to me even now. But he had been clever. He moved from Wales soon after us, and ended up living and working near my family. More to the point, he had won my parents over; he had won everyone over, apart from me, but I was filled with such fear of him that he knew I would never speak up. And if I did, I knew nobody would believe me above him. He had seen to that with great skill, and he continued to be crafty in the way he presented himself to my family. He would bring presents to the house – gifts for my mum, which would be gratefully accepted, and gifts for me. Naturally I would be churlish, not wanting to accept anything from him; and so to those who did not know what he had done I must have seemed very ungrateful. Increasingly he appeared good-natured while I seemed to be a rather unpleasant little girl. It was all going according to his plan.

The first night he babysat, my fears became a horrible reality.

All day I knew that he was going to babysit that evening as Stuart and Sean would be out with friends. I longed for the day to pass slowly, but of course it didn't: almost before I knew it Mum was kissing us good night and telling us to behave well for our babysitter. And then she was gone, and we were alone in the house with him.

It did not happen immediately – he waited for a while before making his move, presumably to make sure that Mum would not come back, having forgotten something. I stayed out of his way, hot fear rising in my chest, praying desperately that my anxieties would prove unfounded. But when it became clear that Mum had genuinely left for the evening, it began.

The first thing Graham did was send Mandy to bed.

I stood in the kitchen, too terrified even to move. With a crushing certainty, I knew what was about to happen. My mouth turned dry and I struggled to stop my body from shaking as I waited for his call. He did not come to get me immediately, however. First he went to the stereo and put on a cassette tape he had brought with him. The music started playing – a song called 'Almost Human'. It was a loud, noisy, aggressive rock song, angry to my ears, with pounding drums and wailing, scary guitars. I would grow to loathe the sound of that song more than anything else, because he would play it every time the abuse was about to start. It was his signature song – a diabolical musical prelude to everything that was to come.

And then he was there. 'You,' he pointed at me with a sneer. 'Come with me.'

Sickness rising in my gut, I followed him as he led me to my room. He didn't say what he was about to do; he didn't even hint anything. But I knew. I realised then that what I had suspected over the past weeks was true: my respite had been just that – a temporary pause while he waited for the moment to be right again.

Once we were in the bedroom he shut the door behind us, then told me to remove my clothes. I shook my head, but one look from him told me that to disobey his order would only make things worse for me so I did as he said.

'Get on the bed, J-J,' he told me.

Sobbing now, I lay down.

He pulled down his trousers and stood over me, semi-naked. I could not bear to look at his body, so instead my eyes were directed towards his face and the steely, implacable wickedness I saw in his eyes.

'Please, don't,' I begged. 'I don't like it. I don't want to do it again.'

His lip curled into an expression of contempt, and I realised that there was no way he was going to stop now. He bent over, lay on top of me and it began.

The second time he raped me was worse than the first, because I knew what was going to happen. The first time he had abused me had been in the middle of the night, and I had been woken up by his actions. This time, I didn't have the luxury of being half asleep and every second of the time I spent on the bed with him that night burned into my brain. What I remember most was how much it hurt as he forced my reluctant legs apart. I tried to resist it, of course, but he was much too strong for me, and my struggling just made matters worse. He held my legs ferociously tightly, his fingernails digging into the skin, and the angry shriek of my hip joints was matched by the scream of pain that escaped my lips – a sickening, heartfelt scream that would have alerted anyone in the vicinity had it been allowed to continue. Graham wasn't going to let that happen, though. He didn't even flinch when I shouted. He just put his hand over my mouth, much as he had done the previous time, muffling my yells and stifling my sobbing breath, then continued to do what he had been planning to do for so long. All the while, the strains of the music he had put on were echoing in my ears and urging him on to new heights of viciousness and brutality.

As I silently put my clothes back on he fetched a small yellow canister of lighter fluid.

'What's that?' I asked him in a small voice.

'I'll show you,' he said. He did not sound like someone who had just brutally raped an eight-year-old girl – his voice was level and calm. Gently he squeezed a little bit of lighter fluid on to the edge of the dressing table then took a box of matches from his pocket, lit one and held it to the fluid. I watched in rapt attention as the lighter fluid burst briefly into flame, before petering out into nothingness.

He gave me a piercing stare. 'That's what happens,' he said, 'when you put a match to lighter fluid.'

I nodded my head. For some strange reason, I felt as though I needed to act like an obedient pupil in a school room. This person had just raped me, and yet here he was acting like a teacher, teaching me something new. Perhaps it was just that I wanted to pretend that nothing had happened; I just wanted to go back to being an ordinary little girl so I obediently allowed myself to be given this little lesson. I had to show enthusiasm. I had to show him I was grateful for the way he was teaching me. I guess I knew what he was capable of if I angered him.

At least I thought I did; but I could never have predicted what happened next.

Suddenly, he grabbed my hand. I gasped, and watched in genuine terror as he squirted some of the flammable liquid on to my skin. Then he let go.

I watched, aghast, as he took the box of matches again and then lit one.

He fixed me with a deadly stare.

'If you ever tell anyone, you dirty little bitch,' he told me, his voice flat and emotionless, 'I will burn you alive, and you will die.'

I watched the flame flickering in his hand as I felt all my strength sap from my muscles in fear. 'I won't tell anyone, Graham,' I stuttered, doing my best to sound convincing and persuasive. 'I promise I won't tell.'

He didn't take his eyes from mine, but he moved the flame fractionally closer towards me.

'Don't!' I begged him, barely able to speak with sudden panic. 'I promise I won't tell.'

For a moment he did nothing; then he nodded with satisfaction, turned and blew out the match.

I had no reason to believe that this man who had insinuated his way into our house was not telling the truth. I believed him. He had shown me how easily the lighter fluid burned; he had squirted some on to my skin. What was there to stop him from now burning me alive?

'You'd better not,' he told me spitefully. He stood up, then grabbed the lighter fluid and meaningfully put it into his pocket before turning and leaving the room. I stood up painfully, my tummy aching once more from what he had just done, then crept on to my bed, curled up into a little ball, and cried, and cried, and cried.

Now that it had started once more, I did not think that it would ever, ever stop.

# 4
# *Playing Jackie*

He called it 'playing Jackie'.

Jackie was the name of an auntie of mine, and for some weird, childlike reason I hated saying her name. I had no problem with Jackie herself, but there was something about the sound of the word that I didn't like, and it became something of a joke in the family. Graham picked up on this, and as he did with so many things, twisted it to his own purpose. And if the word Jackie was unpleasant to my ears beforehand, it was doubly so now.

'We're going to play Jackie tonight, J-J,' Graham would whisper.

I would shake my head. 'I don't want to play,' I would shudder.

'Oh, yeah. You've got to play Jackie.'

And play Jackie we would, whenever he wanted. It meant nothing to him that I didn't like the game, and the rules were always what he decided they were to be.

'Jackie' was not the sort of game any child would have wanted to play; but maybe if there were other, more normal kids' games for me to lose myself in, it would have been easier to deal with. I was to find that difficult as well, however.

Being a poor Irish kid in the comfortable corner of middle England in which we found ourselves was not easy. Perhaps we shouldn't have longed for the burned-out cars and the ragged kids; but I found myself missing them, stuck in a place where I didn't belong. Shouts of 'Fucking Paddys, go back to where you came from,' were not uncommon; and it wasn't long before I realised that the bold signs in pub windows stating 'No Travellers' were actually referring to us. We weren't like all the posh people we found ourselves living amongst; our neighbours and others had no qualms about making us feel like outcasts, and so many of them were antisocial and unfriendly. I naturally spoke with a thick Belfast accent that made it clear to anyone who heard my voice that I was not from those parts, and the other children at my new school instantly picked up on that.

The walk to school was very beautiful – a lovely, scenic route that took me through areas of lush greenery and parkland, a far cry from the longed-for, bombed-out environment of my former home. I would have to walk past a lake where I could spot little frogs and other wildlife, which I always liked. But the attractive journey was a stark contrast to the apprehension I would feel when I made my way to school. I was the new kid, I was different – and when you're young, being different is not a good thing. Children being what they are, I was immediately targeted by the bullies. It was not only the girls who would give me a hard time, but also the boys.

It would always start with the chants. I would hear the taunts on my way to school coming from the various gangs of kids that had chosen to pick on me. 'We don't want no fucking Irish people in our country,' they would shout. 'Get out!' I wanted to try and explain to them that I wasn't Irish, I was English, that I was the same as they were; but I didn't have the courage or the sophistication to do that, and I don't suppose it would have done much good anyway. When people want somebody to bully, they generally don't listen to reason.

Other times they would approach me with false smiles and ask me to say a particular word or phrase. I had to do what they said to avoid an instant beating, but the moment I pronounced – or, to their ears, mispronounced – the word they had given me they would shriek with laughter and use my supposed ignorance as an excuse to start with the bullying. More often than not someone would grab a clump of my hair in their fist, pull and twist it hard, then start yelling at me: 'You're so *stupid*! You're a *spastic*!' I heard that one word – 'spastic' – more often than I could count, every day, while I was being poked and kicked and punched by everyone. They would pass me round so they could all have a go.

When they were feeling more aggressive, they would call me 'Irish scum'. Sometimes I would be held down while one of my classmates rubbed the ground-up crumbs of dried leaves into my face and hair; on other occasions I would be fiercely kicked in the legs as I tried to make my way into school so that my shins were bruised and sore. They would even steal my school bag and throw it into the lake so that my school work and books became saturated and unusable. Once they even attached a dog collar to my neck and started dragging me around.

I wouldn't even be given any respite when I got to the supposed sanctuary of the school buildings. When I arrived at the gates, there would always be prefects there in charge of making sure everyone kept in line and arrived at school on time. They saw their duties towards me, however, as being somewhat different. I would always turn up to school in good time, but they would hold me at the gate. 'You're not going in,' they would say.

'Why not?' I always asked, though I knew what their reply would be.

'Cos we say so,' they would tell me spitefully. 'We think you're up to something because you're Irish. All you thieving Paddys ever do is steal and be bad. We know what you're like.'

They would grin at each other, then physically restrain me so that, no matter how hard I struggled, I didn't get to my classroom on time. Lateness was frowned upon at that school, and they knew perfectly well what their actions would mean: a late mark, the punishment for which was being given the slipper in front of the whole school. I was late so often, and ever reluctant to say why, that I must have seemed to my teachers like a very disobedient, surly little girl, in much the same way as I must have seemed at home. And as this was in the days when corporal punishment was commonplace, more often than not I would be pulled up on to the stage in front of all these children in this strange town, to be beaten with a slipper by one of the teachers, aware all the while of the sniggers of the other pupils watching me. Invariably the hot flush of shame and humiliation was worse than the actual pain of the beating, although the pain was bad enough.

I remember coming home once in floods of tears, humiliated and aching from the beatings. I knew Mum would be in the house, though, so before I walked in I tried to compose myself and wiped the tears from my face with my sleeve. My skin, raw from crying, hurt as I did so. I walked into the house and sat down in the kitchen, my school bag trailing behind me. I said nothing as Mum went about her business.

'What's the matter, Jayne?' Mum asked.

I stared down at the table. 'Nothing,' I replied quietly. I didn't want her to see the state I had been in because by then I was so worried that people would think it was me that had been bad. I could feel tears welling up into my eyes, so I grabbed my school bag and went up to my room, where I could cry undisturbed. I could never understand the hatred I was shown, but there was nothing I could do but resign myself to it and accept that that was the way it was going to be. There was no other route I could take to school to avoid the taunts, and it would be useless trying to arrive earlier because the prefects would always be at the gate and would just hold me there until I was late. And my word against theirs was never going to be believed.

The only person that knew what I was going through was Stuart, because once again he was encountering the same treatment. He was only little for his age, so on the surface he was an easy target for most of the kids he came into contact with, especially as they went around in gangs. Boys would hang around after school waiting for him just so that they could beat him up. Whole groups of them would lay into him, kicking and punching him, spitting in his face, laughing at him and calling him 'scum'. It was so humiliating for both of us.

It was a little different for Stuart than it was for me, however. He was older, for a start, and he had gone through the exact same experience when we moved from England to Ireland all those years ago. Unlike me, he had a strategy to deal with it: when he was being attacked, he would curl up into a little ball and take the blows to his body without once crying or showing any sign of weakness. And when the time was right, he fought back. After living in Northern Ireland, he was an accomplished fighter, and soon his contemporaries grew to learn that he was not someone to mess with. I wasn't like that, however. I hated violence; I hated confrontation; I didn't want to cause any trouble; I was at the opposite end of the scale to Stuart. And so the bullying got worse because I never told anyone about what was happening – all I could do was put up with it. Even then I was struck by the irony of it: I had moved from Ireland, with its bombs and guns and street violence, to a sleepy corner of England; yet here I was at the receiving end of more violence and unpleasantness than I could have imagined. I longed to go back more than ever.

Sometimes, though, I would have Stuart by my side. Once he had established himself, having him with me meant that my trips to school were transformed. He would wait outside school for me; if I was given any aggro, he would shout at my bullies to 'fuck off', and his presence seemed to keep them at bay. I think he knew how much it meant to me to be able to spend time with him: sometimes, on these occasions, he would take me on little outings, like he had done in Ireland. Often we would go and play by the lake. We enjoyed fishing. Of course, we didn't have real fishing rods, but Stuart would fashion makeshift ones using sticks, wire and plastic bags. I'll never forget the first time I caught a fish on one of these after-school expeditions. I desperately wanted to take it home to show my mum, but Stuart wasn't having any of it. 'You can't do that, Jayne,' he told me.

'Why not, Stu?'

'Because it will die,' he said. Tenderly he took my plastic bag full of lake water. 'You have to let them straight back in,' he said quietly, before releasing the tiny, silvery fish back into the water, then making up for my disappointment by taking me by the hand and leading me to a patch of water where he knew there was some frogspawn. 'We'll take some of this home,' he said, 'and in a few days it'll turn into lots of baby frogs.'

This was a new wonder to me. Despite what was going on at home, I had no idea where any kind of baby, let alone baby frogs, came from. Wide-eyed, I helped him fill a bucket and we took it home. Sure enough, some time later, the frogspawn turned to tadpoles and then frogs: Stuart solicitously insisted that we gather all the babies up and take them back to the lake where they would be safe.

But life was not always so idyllic. One day, a group of children had been particularly evil to me, and I told my brother about it. A grim look passed his face, and he told me he would deal with the situation. He was like a different person from the gentle boy who had released the baby frogs back into the wild. I felt a mixture of excitement and apprehension. I was glad that there was somebody there who might be able to do something about the bullying, but I knew that Stuart would stop at nothing to protect me, and I didn't want him to go too far. I didn't want anyone to get hurt; I simply wanted to be left alone.

'Don't hit them, Stu,' I told him.

Stuart shook his head. 'They've been hitting you,' he said bleakly. 'It's got to be dealt with. They've got to be punished.'

'No, but don't *hit* them,' I pleaded. Even then I knew that I didn't want any violence to be done in my name. All I wanted was for them to have some small understanding of the fear that they had put me through.

Stuart wasn't having it. He walked with me to school that morning and made me point out the group of kids who had been the nastiest of all. 'But *please* don't hit anyone,' I repeated.

He ignored me, strolled straight over to them and immediately grabbed the biggest boy among them. Without a word, he landed a heavy punch on the boy's mouth, and his lip immediately split in a torrent of blood.

'Stuart!' I screamed. 'Don't!'

My brother turned round, and for a brief second I saw

anger in his face. He wiped the boy's blood from his fist, then answered me. 'Don't tell me what I can and can't do,' he shouted, his voice firmer than I had ever heard it. 'Don't interfere with this kind of business. Keep out of it.'

The whole thing had gone far further than I wanted it to, but I have to admit to a sense of satisfaction when I saw the rest of the group of kids run away. Normally it would have been me who wanted to escape; now the tables had turned, and even though I was shaking from the sight I had just witnessed, I felt relief that, for one day at least, I wouldn't have to undergo the torment of bullying.

After that, the bullying started to ease off. I even found that some of the girls who had been the ringleaders would approach me with a much friendlier tone of voice, and rather than start trying to provoke a reaction out of me, they would smile and talk normally to me. It was a sudden hand of friendship that surprised and gladdened me, but it wasn't to last. I don't know if word of what Stuart had done got out, but the mothers of those two girls started coming to school with them. The first time they saw me, they singled me out.

'We don't want you to have anything to do with those travellers, all right?' they said to their daughters, their voices angry, and I could immediately see the fear that they instilled in them. And so my new-found school friendships were over almost before they were begun, and I found it nearly impossible to make any more friends. And so the loneliness was back as quickly as it had disappeared.

As much as I dreaded going to school, however, it did at least mean one thing: I wasn't at home.

That place had now become somewhere I associated in my mind with Graham's sickening abuse, which continued any time he babysat. In my memories of that time, he always seemed to be there. It can't have been the case; he might have been the babysitter but he wasn't part of our immediate family and it wasn't as if he lived with us. But it was certainly the case that the more time passed, the more he insinuated his way into our little unit, a wolf in sheep's clothing if ever there was one, always wanting to 'play Jackie' with me.

His very presence nauseated me. And it wasn't just the ever-present, nagging threat of sexual abuse that I found traumatising; there was a constant barrage of emotional abuse that went with it. Spiteful comments, barely veiled threats – he would use any words he could find to break my willpower and ensure that I was always compliant. Of course, he would never say anything untoward when my family could hear – my parents and either of my brothers would have gone mad if they had had any idea of what was going on – but when he was there, in any quiet moment out of the earshot of the others he would whisper hateful things at me, reminding me what a dirty, hated and unloved little girl I was; how I was a liar and a bitch; telling me what he would do to me if I ever spoke a word of anything to anyone. His green eyes would flash as he did so, and with a horrible tingle I would remember the sight of the lighter fluid, burning on the dressing table in my bedroom with its silent yellow-blue flame. In bed at night I would wonder what it would be like to be burned alive.

When we were alone in the house, not doing what he told me to do would be unthinkable; but he still found ways to strengthen his hold over me. When Mum went out, she would always make sure that there was food in the fridge, leaving instructions with Graham about what we should have for our tea. Characteristically, however, he would use *my* food as another weapon against me. Sometimes he would call to me that my tea was ready; I would go into the kitchen to find that he had prepared me a piece of toast, burned to an inedible crisp, with nothing to drink. Refusing to eat it was obviously not an option, and he would look over me with a cruel smile as I tried to force the dry, charcoaled food down my throat, feeling like I was going to choke on it, but knowing that it was the only thing I was likely to get to eat. It didn't take long, however, for him to think of a different way to use food as a means to get me to do what he wanted.

One day, quite early on, Mum went out to work. Dad had already left on business the previous morning, my brothers were both out and Graham had been left in charge. With the sensation of gruesome apprehension that I had quickly become used to, I heard the door slam shut, and the house fall silent. How I had learned to hate that silence: the calm before the storm. I sat in my bedroom, reading a book or playing with a toy, desperately trying to persuade myself that tonight nothing would happen. Soon enough, however, I heard the footsteps approaching, and the door opening. I didn't look up as he walked in – I just sat there concentrating, or appearing to concentrate, on whatever I was doing.

He stood there quietly for a minute before speaking. 'Hungry, J-J?' he asked.

Without looking at him, I nodded my head. 'Yeah.'

There was a pause. 'Well, there's no tea for you tonight.'

I felt a chill. Something different was about to happen, but I didn't know what. 'But I'm hungry,' I said.

He stepped towards me. 'Well, maybe I'll be nice,' he said. There was a slight tremor in his voice as he spoke. 'But you'll have to do something for me.'

I didn't understand. If he was going to rape me, there was never usually this preamble; and I knew that 'something nice' for him was unlikely to be something nice for me.

I clenched my teeth as I saw him undressing. His belt buckle clunked as he undid it, then slithered as he slid the leather through the metal. I tried to think of other things, but I knew what was coming.

'We're going to do something different today,' he told me.

I didn't reply.

He pulled me towards him, then pushed my hand downwards.

I started to struggle. 'No!' I complained. 'I don't want to. I don't want to do that. Don't make me touch it.'

But I didn't have any choice. His grip was strong. It was the first time he had instructed me to use my hand on him, to keep doing it until he had finished, and the act made me want to be sick. Of all the things he made me do, that was perhaps the most awful. Of course, that meant nothing to Graham, and before long I found myself doing that more often than anything else.

It disgusted me, having to touch him in that way, having to be the one that was doing something to him. Of course, I didn't really know what I was meant to do, but he soon showed me how to do it the way he liked it. I couldn't bear to look, so I kept my gaze averted; but that didn't seem to worry him. Even now, as I did then, I find it impossible to understand how someone can take pleasure from that when they know that they are forcing an unwilling partner into being involved – forcing someone who would rather be anywhere in the whole world than doing that one thing to them. There was no way he could have been in any doubt that I was repulsed by what he was making me do, but he seemed to thrive on that repulsion. He seemed to love it.

The memory of being a little girl having to do such things makes such a sensation of shame and nausea rise up in me that I can hardly bear to recall it. But Graham must have enjoyed what I was doing, because I lost count of how often I had to earn the right to eat my supper by performing that hateful task. 'Please don't make me do this,' I would beg, feeling sick at the thought of what was about to happen. But my pleas fell on deaf ears; I am sure my begging actually added to his enjoyment.

While things were going from bad to worse for me, the rest of the family seemed to be settling into their new life. Mum in particular seemed to be socialising a bit more. It did her a lot of good, I think, to be able to go out to work, and now and then she even went out to the local bingo hall. Had she known the price at which her new-found freedom was bought, no doubt she would never have left me alone again; but she didn't, and I watched her blossom as the chains of domestic drudgery were slightly loosened. With Dad away so often with work, it was great that she was getting out and about making new friends and having some fun. Stuart and Sean settled in well too, making plenty of friends, which meant that they were often out of the home in the early evenings when the abuse would normally occur.

While I did not see much of Sean, it was Stuart who I really missed. We had a bond, and I knew he would do anything for me – I only had to ask. But I never had the voice, or the words, or the bravery to do so, and so – like everyone else in my family – Stuart simply assumed that all was well.

But all was not well: the abuse continued, and gradually it seemed to become a normal part of my life, like brushing my teeth or going to school. I would hear the front door slam shut, I would be called by his ugly voice and the music would start pounding out from the stereo. I would only have to hear the opening few bars of 'Almost Human' to know what was round the corner: each beat of the drum was like a desperate pounding of my heart, and the lyrics would seem to echo in my head for hours, sometimes days, afterwards.

It wasn't too long after the second time he raped me that he decided to take me out of my bedroom and into my parents'. I didn't understand why at first, but then I realised that it was because there was a lock on the door: with me securely locked in Mum and Dad's room with him, he could do whatever he wanted to. There was also a mirror opposite the bed – I don't know whether he got excited or not from seeing a reflection of what was happening. I think he probably did.

And so my life began to take shape, moulded by his incessant, twisted, sexual needs. How I dealt with it I couldn't say – I guess that even when you are young, you find resources within yourself to cope with the most terrible situations. Every morning when he was to babysit I would wake up expecting that, when evening arrived, I would have to do something for him, or have something done to me. I would be bullied at school, or, at the very best, simply ignored, but the way the other children treated me seemed to pale into insignificance compared to the other trouble in my life. The seconds would tick excruciatingly by in the schoolroom as I waited to find out what my early-evening torture would be. Sometimes I had a reprieve if Sean or Stuart happened not to be out as planned, or Mum wasn't working or if Dad returned early from one of his work trips – how I loved the days when that was the case. Occasionally Graham didn't put me through hell. But even if a visit passed without any abuse, it was barely a relief; I knew that it was just a matter of time before I would be required to go into Mum and Dad's room, and it would start all over again.

The weeks turned to months; soon I became almost numb to it: I reached the stage where rather than being overcome with dread every time I knew it was about to happen, I learned simply to steel myself against it, knowing that the sooner he did whatever particular perversion was in his mind on that day, the sooner it would be over and I could go to bed to cry myself to sleep. And just as my attitude towards our evening encounters changed, so did his. Gradually the actual physical rapes started to become marginally less frequent; they still happened, of course, but now he had a new game: pornography. He would bring pornographic magazines to the house. While I was locked in Mum and Dad's bedroom with him, he would spread them out so that I was surrounded by disgusting images that I simply could not bear to look at; and yet he would make me look at them while I was doing the things he instructed me to do. The images of naked women all around me would be blurred by the tears in my eyes.

While the sexual abuse changed gradually over time, the verbal abuse did not. Whenever we were alone, he would repeat his threats to me. I was a disgusting bitch, a dirty liar. If I ever tried to tell anyone, he would kill me. More than once he demonstrated for me again his trick with the lighter fluid, sprinkling the stinking liquid on my skin then waving a flickering match in my direction until I was weak with fear. Even if I did tell anyone, he would remind me, they wouldn't believe me.

'You never told the first time,' he would say with an unpleasant leer. 'They'll think you're guilty. They'll think it's all your fault. They'll think you like it.' And I knew he was right. Everyone seemed to regard him as wonderful, and in my mind I believed that I was thought of as nothing but a spoiled and naughty little girl. I was dirty. I was bad. I deserved what happened to me. I would never tell anyone, apart from in my silent and heartfelt prayers, which continued every night as I thanked God for the fact that Graham had not yet killed me. I understood God could not stop Graham from raping me, but I begged Him to stop my abuser hurting me, or at least not hurt me much; I begged Him to keep me safe. Those night-time prayers were a small comfort to me, and when I had finished them, I would feel a little bit stronger. I would try to think happy thoughts – thoughts of Ireland and how, when I was old enough, I would go back there to escape him. But I never did.

There were times when I thought that if I could guarantee it would be painless, I would rather die than carry on suffering everything that Graham inflicted upon me. But at the same time, I knew that dying would mean leaving my mum and dad, and I didn't want to do that. It was a fear he tapped into. More than once, he would say to me, 'You tell anyone, J-J, and you'll never see your mum and dad again. You know that, don't you? It will be the end for you.'

I would nod my head in mute agreement, tears gathering in the corner of my eyes.

As the weeks turned into months, I became fractionally braver. Not brave enough to reveal to anyone what was going on, certainly; but at least brave enough to feel the stirrings of rebellion in my bruised gut. The abuse had been going on for nearly a year the first time I tried to stand up to him.

I had woken up that morning with a sense of purpose. The abuse he had been inflicting on me over the past few occasions had been particularly unpleasant, even by his brutal standards, and something in me had changed. All that day at school, and the next, I found myself gathering courage, almost subconsciously at first, but then with a vigour that was uncharacteristic for me. Why should I have to do these things for him? What if I just said no? I put from my thoughts all images of the burning lighter fluid, and in the optimistic light of day I even found myself bravely discounting his repeated threats that echoed in my mind over and over, like the after-ring of an ugly bell.

That night he was to stay over. This didn't happen very often – only if Dad was away overnight on a trip and Mum was going to be back particularly late – but I knew when it did that I could probably expect something especially vicious. Often, when he stayed, I would be raped twice in one evening depending on what time Sean and Stuart got back; and when I heard the door slamming as my mum went to work, I felt a sense of foreboding that this was going to be an especially cruel night.

As usual, Mandy was asleep; 'Almost Human' started

playing on the hi-fi. And then he was there, nodding at me to get into my parents' room – there was no longer any need for words, as I knew perfectly well what I was expected to do. There was no question of me doing anything other than obeying.

Except that night, I had other plans.

I shook my head. 'I don't want to,' I mumbled.

'What?'

'I said, I don't want to,' I repeated, a little more forcefully this time.

His face remained expressionless as I tried to stare him down. I didn't realise it at that moment, but he was considering what my punishment was to be for defying him.

I have a terrible fear of enclosed spaces, and always have done, ever since I was tiny. There was no way Graham could have known that, so it was just my bad luck he came up with the most terrible torture he could have devised for me. I guess when you are evil you just have a feel for these things.

First he approached me, grabbed my hair and pulled it hard. I gasped in pain, but he didn't stop – he just kept pulling until great clumps of it started to come away and fall on the carpet. It hurt more than I can describe. He threw me roughly to the floor, where I collapsed, holding my head in unbelievable agony thinking this was the moment I would die, while he found a sleeping bag, and forced me on pain of violence to get inside. Tears welling in my eyes, I shook my head.

'Get inside,' he repeated.

'I'm sorry,' I whimpered. 'I'm so sorry. Please don't make me . . .' My whole body was shaking, but the more I begged him not to make me get into the sleeping bag, the more he insisted.

I did as I was told, but then he started pushing my sore head into the bag, then kicking the rest of me inside. I struggled and wriggled, but I wasn't strong enough to stop him. Immediately I felt constricted when suddenly, to my horror, I realised that he was tying up the top of the sleeping bag to keep me trapped inside. I struggled even more desperately, but without success: there was no way I was going to get out of there until he untied me.

It soon grew unbearably hot and airless in that sleeping bag. I entered a state of appalling panic, my limbs shaking as I started gasping for air. But there wasn't any, and instead I found myself trying to inhale mouthfuls of the sleeping-bag fabric. My breathing started to sound like an animal – big, rasping gulps, as if I was suffocating. All my fears of being enclosed crashed in on me. I felt as if I was being buried alive, or crushed to death, my lungs stuffed with cotton wool. I have no idea how long he kept me inside that sleeping bag, but it was a long time; when finally he let me out, I was a sobbing, distraught wreck. He had made his point with characteristic brutality and I realised I didn't have the right to say no. He was in charge.

But my punishment didn't end there.

That night I cried myself to sleep as usual; but when I awoke the following morning, I could immediately sense that something was not right. My face was sore, and there was a dreadful, stinking smell in my room, on me. It was early, and there was nobody else awake, so I crept out of my bed and made my way to the bathroom. When I looked in the mirror, I was horrified by what I saw. My abuser had crept in while I slept and had smeared his own excrement over my face. It was still there, and my skin had become sore and pimpled as a result. With a whimper I scrubbed it off immediately, feeling more soiled and dirty than I ever had done in my life. It hurt to rub my face so hard, but I didn't care – I just wanted vigorously to remove all trace of him.

Once I was clean, I went back to my bedroom. The unpleasant smell was still there, and it was coming from my bed. I investigated further and realised that the bedclothes were damp. I knew for sure I had not wet the bed that night, and it suddenly became clear to me what he had done.

As a further punishment for my rebelliousness, he had entered my room as I slept and urinated over me. It was something he was to repeat on a number of occasions after that.

He would do anything, it seemed, to make sure I remained bent to his will for as long as he wanted his soul-destroying abuse to continue.

At school I became known as the smelly kid, and not without reason. There was a smell that lingered around me.

It wasn't for want of washing myself. In addition to my usual routine, I would scrub myself down every time he abused me. Sometimes rough soap and a flannel or brush did not seem like enough to wash away the dirty feeling I was left with after I had been with him, and so I started to use bleach, watering it down slightly in the bathroom sink and sluicing it over my skin before scrubbing hard and trying to imagine that it was doing some sort of good in cleaning his filth away from me.

But for some children, even that level of washing is not enough. Graham's abuse would generally happen in the early evening before I went to bed. But that didn't mean I would feel safe once bedtime had arrived – far from it. I would lie under the covers terrified that he would visit me again before Mum got back from work and he had to go home. And so I started to wet the bed – sometimes because I was simply too afraid to get out and go to the bathroom in case I met him and he decided to inflict more abuse upon me, but more often as a kind of defence against his attentions. With my child's logic, I calculated that he would not want anything to do with me if I smelled of wee.

Mum was upset that I had started to wet the bed again at such a late age, and she would get a bit angry with me. I was told that I was not allowed to have a drink before I went to bed, but of course that didn't stop me from doing it, and each time my sheets were wet she would become more and more frustrated.

'Did you have a drink before you went to bed, Jayne?' she would demand.

'No, Mum,' I would reply weakly.

'Well, you're old enough not to do this any more,' she would tell me. 'It's smelly and you should know better.'

I was disappointing her, I knew that. But of course I couldn't tell her why it was happening, and so I had to endure her telling off. Once, she didn't change the sheets immediately – perhaps her way of trying to stop me doing it, but it only made me smellier.

Dad had a different technique when he returned from work.

'Stop wetting the bed, Jayne,' he'd tell me, 'and I'll give you ten pence.'

He could have offered me all the riches in the world. I would never have stopped.

My bed-wetting plan didn't really work, however. If Graham decided not to visit me after bedtime, it was because his desires had been satisfied; on the occasions that they hadn't, the fact that I had wet the bed did not stop him. *Nothing* stopped him. But no matter how well I washed myself, the aroma of urine would cling to me during the daytime, giving my schoolmates an excuse to taunt and tease me.

It was hellish. Despite the relentless playground teasing, outside of school I did my best to remain cheerful and sunny. It was so hard, and I didn't always manage it, but I tried my best. In fact, my uncles and aunties who sometimes came to visit started to call me Cinderella. I was so eager to please, so eager to prove that I wasn't the nasty little girl that I thought people suspected, that I would get up early in the morning and prepare the fireplace, getting rid of the previous night's hot coals and laying a new fire for when Mum came down; I would help clean the house; I would peel the vegetables for Sunday dinner; I would help my dad in the garden. I seemed to really enjoy keeping busy; but looking back I wonder if it wasn't a coping mechanism, a way of allowing me to keep my mind off the horror of my situation.

I had other ways of coping, too. I used to wander all by myself to the fields near our house and watch the frogs and the lizards and the grass snakes – I was so fascinated by what I could find in the natural world, and loved being alone with whatever wildlife I could find. For short periods of time it would allow my attention to be diverted and distract me from everything else.

All little children need someone to talk to, someone to listen to their problems and their fears, no matter how small or silly they might seem in the grand scheme of things. But when you're told on an almost daily basis that you are bad and dirty, a liar and a bitch, you become too scared to have these conversations. I didn't want to be judged for what was happening to me; I didn't want to be told off; I didn't want anybody to think I had been bad. And so I continued not to tell my parents or brothers what was happening; I continued to keep it my shameful, hated secret.

But I needed an outlet. I needed to voice my frustrations in some way. As a family pet, we had a little Yorkshire terrier – a rescue dog from Battersea Dogs' Home – whom we called Pepper. Pepper became my confidante, my shoulder to cry on, my friend. I told her everything – all the things that Graham was doing to me, how I knew he would kill me if I told anyone and how nobody would believe me anyway. I shared my secrets with that little dog, knowing that she, at least, would not judge me for what I had done. She couldn't answer back, she couldn't tell me off, she couldn't punish me – all she did was listen patiently. She would lie on my bed, put her little paw on my face and comfort me. From an adult perspective it seems ridiculous, but at the time I honestly believed that she understood every word I said. It was our little secret, and she knew I'd get in trouble if I told anyone. I *had* to believe it. I had to think that I was sharing my problems in some way, otherwise I think I would have gone mad. It was a small thing, but in my childlike world Pepper became enormously important to me, and I would talk to her of what was happening whenever I knew I could do so without being overheard.

But Pepper was just a dog, and while she could absorb whatever worries I chose to tell her, she couldn't stop the abuse from continuing. I had to find other ways of dealing with it in my mind. In my bedroom was a cupboard where I had a small collection of dolls and toy furniture. Whenever I was feeling sad, I would take my dolls out of their place and use them to enact what to my mind was a perfect family scene: a mum, a dad, two children, all living happily, all living without the shadow under which I found myself. I could escape into the idyllic world of those dolls for hours at a time, using my imagination to press the reality of my life out of my mind. I envied my dolls, envied the scene I had created for them. One day, I would tell myself, I will have everything that they have.

But until that time, I had real life to contend with. Real life was not like the life my dollies lived in their dolls' house, and real families were not like the ones I fantasised about, no matter how much I wanted them to be.

As time passed, and I grew a little older, I was allowed to go outside to play for a while in the evenings. I even made myself a real friend – Virginia – who, unlike the kids at school, seemed to see past everything else and was content to have me in her company. She was three or four years older than me and came from a good, well-to-do family. Her parents were better off than mine, and her mum and dad seemed so glamorous to me. Simply going down to the pub like my parents did wasn't for them; they had more extravagant diversions, like dinner-dances and balls, the sort of things that seemed a million miles away from our little life. I remember seeing Virginia's mum dressed in an elaborate ball gown, all satin and sequins, and thinking she looked more glamorous than anyone I had ever seen; and when Virginia was invited to a fancy-dress party she was dressed up in the most fabulous Little Bo Peep outfit I had ever seen. They seemed like the perfect family – like the family that I had enacted with my dolls during the darkest moments of Graham's abuse – and while I knew that my own family would never be like that, at least it was something to aspire to, and I worked on my friendship with Virginia as hard as I could. Luckily for me, despite the age gap between us, my friendship was reciprocated. She appeared to really like me just for being me.

During those precious moments of outside play, we would do standard kids' things – playing in the street, sharing secrets. Sometimes I would go to her house; less often she would come to mine. It was good to have a friend after all that I had been through. I was strictly forbidden to stay out beyond a certain time when Graham was coming round to babysit however, and was meticulous about not breaking the rules as I knew that Graham's response would have been characteristically severe.

The front room of our house looked out on to the street where we lived. It was a big, wide window, but obscured by the thick net curtains that were fashionable back then. I had been playing happily outside with Virginia when I realised that I had forgotten about the time: I had no watch, and with a small lurch of my stomach, I told my friend that I had better go and see if it was time for me to go inside yet, as I was supposed to be back by 5 p.m. Virginia nodded, and I ran to the front window of the house.

I knew what I was looking for: we had a clock on the wall that was trendy at the time, but I suppose if I were to see it again now I'd find it quite ugly. But it was large and could be read from outside, and I always used it to keep track of the time. I peered through the window, straining my eyes through the opaque net curtains to try to see it.

What I actually saw was Graham standing at the window, holding his wrist up and tapping his watch.

The very sight of him made me jump, and I could tell by the look on his face that I was in trouble. My eyes flickered up to the clock on the wall: it was a couple of minutes to five. But when I looked at Graham's watch, it said one minute past.

I went weak with dread. I knew Graham would insist that his watch told the right time and that I was late back; I knew I wasn't clever enough or brave enough to argue with him that clocks sometimes told different times and that maybe his watch was a couple of minutes fast.

I looked over at Virginia. 'I have to go home,' I told her weakly. I think she saw that I was scared about something, because she nodded at me with a quizzical look on her face before walking away.

I opened the door and walked into the house. He was there waiting for me, his wrist still held up meaningfully. 'You're late,' he said.

'I'm sorry,' I replied in a small voice. 'I thought it was . . .'

'You know you're not supposed to be late,' he interrupted me, his voice threatening. 'What do you think I am, a fucking pushover?'

'No,' I whimpered. 'I—'

'Kitchen,' he said. 'Now!'

I scurried into the kitchen. There was no sign of any food for tea, but there was a pile of laundry that had been washed but not yet dried. Mum always had to squeeze the water out of the wet washing by putting it through the rollers of an old-fashioned mangle.

Graham picked up a pair of wet jeans – Stuart's perhaps, or Sean's – and handed them to me.

'Dry them,' he said. 'It's your punishment.'

Confused, I put the jeans to the mangle like I had seen my mum do, then tried to turn the handle to pass them through. But I was nowhere near strong enough, and the rollers ground to a halt within a few seconds. The jeans hung limply from the mangle.

'I can't do it,' I said, my voice choked.

'What do you mean, you can't do it?'

'I just can't.'

His eyes narrowed and flickered towards the mangle. I couldn't stop myself wondering what he had in mind. Was he going to hurt me? To force my fingers in between the rollers and turn the handle? Or would he remove the wet jeans and beat me with them?

Graham himself seemed to be wondering what to do. Finally he spoke.

'Go to your room.'

It was the worst thing he could have said. I knew what it meant.

'Please don't,' I begged him.

'Just go to your room.'

I nodded as tears welled up in my eyes, then scurried away.

I knew he would come. It was just a matter of time. I

think perhaps he enjoyed toying with me, like a cat with a mouse, making me suffer the agony of having to wait for him. I don't know how long I sat there shivering with fear, but before long he was there.

He had brought some magazines with him. Slowly, deliberately, he laid them out on the floor, looking slowly at the pages that pleased him the most. I tried not to stare at the horrible pictures of the centrefolds exposing themselves; but it was a choice between that and having to watch him unbuckle his trousers and pull down his pants.

'You know what to do,' he whispered.

I froze, but one look at his face told me that if I took too long in coming to him, I would regret it, and so I stepped over to where he sat and nervously put my hand around him. He closed his eyes and smiled, then looked back at the magazines he loved so much while I did what he wanted, trying all the time not to be sick.

When it was over, and I had wiped my hands clean of him, he gathered up his magazines and made to leave.

'Don't be late again,' he muttered as he walked out of my room, 'or you know what'll happen.'

But it happened whether I was late or not. There was nothing I could do to stop it.

# 5

# The Mistake

When he was a teenager, I was well aware that Stuart used his skill at fighting to help protect me on more than one occasion. When he dealt with the bullying kids outside school, I watched with a kind of thrilled horror as he laid into these people, not holding back, and displaying the full force of his pent-up aggression as he beat them so severely that I couldn't bear to look.

I had always hated violence. I suppose it came from seeing the horrific way in which Stuart was bullied and beaten up: the events that forced *him* into being a teenage warrior led *me* down a very different path. But when you're young, your emotions are not as clear-cut as that; even now, as an adult, I can recognise that Stuart's unquestioning, unqualified love for his sister led him to perform acts of violence that, if I had looked at them from the outside, I would have condemned. I couldn't look at them from the outside, though. They were about me. They were *for* me. Despite the fact that I never wanted to see people hurt, I loved him all the more for it. He was, quite literally, my saviour.

Violence breeds violence, however. It was obvious to Stuart that his methods were working: the more he fought, the more respect he gained. He never wanted to go back to being the little kid who was taunted and pulverised by his contemporaries, and he believed that the only way to avoid that, the only way to get to the top of the tree, was to fight his way to recognition.

It didn't take long for fighting to become a way of life for him. Sean, too, used to have to fight his way out of trouble, but with Stuart, it always went that bit too far.

It was so strange for me, even as a young girl, to see the different sides to his character. I knew him for what he was. I knew him to be the sweet, loving little boy who would do anything to protect the ones he loved. I knew him to be the kid who had comforted me when I'd been frightened. I knew him to be the person who had stepped in when he found out his little sister had been bullied. I knew him as my guardian angel.

But other people saw a different Stuart. They saw an aggressive boy who seemed to look for fights, who seemed almost keen for someone to challenge him. I wanted to tell everyone the truth, that beneath the rough exterior, beneath the husk that had been hardened by the way other children had treated him, there were sparks of kindness. But it became difficult even for me to stand up for him sometimes. He made no attempt to hide from me the road he was taking. Occasionally I would beg him not to be so aggressive, telling him that one day someone would come along who would really try to hurt him. One day he would lose.

'Like I give a fuck, Jayne,' he would say dismissively, unconcerned about the language he was using in front of someone so young. 'You don't lose a fight, you just come second. I've kicked the shit out of some of the best bastards in this shit hole.' His language would get increasingly bad the more he warmed to his subject. 'Age and size is fuck all, it's just a fucking illusion. I'll take them all on – I don't care.'

As time passed, Stuart veered further off the rails. I suppose he had been obliged to fight ever since he was a little boy, and now it was a habit for him: he had been bullied once too often, and fighting back had become a matter of routine. He started bunking off school with his ever-increasing circle of friends, hanging around the town drinking bottles of cheap cider, dossing round at friends' houses, getting drunk. Nothing could really persuade him to go to school, and he certainly couldn't care less about education. The system had failed my brother, so he turned his back on it. 'Fuck 'em,' was all he would ever say about the matter.

Deep down, though, Stuart knew what was happening to him. He would have moments of startling honesty when we were together, moments when he admitted he knew he was on the wrong road. 'I don't want to be like this, Jayne,' he told me once. He admitted that he hated growing up around so much violence, especially when he thought back to the general horrors he had seen on the streets in Northern Ireland, that it had made his skin crawl when he was a little boy and he never wanted it to be part of his life; but, he told me, he hadn't had a choice. Fighting back had been the only way he could survive, and that way of life had taken him over.

When I heard him say these things, it only half made sense to me. But even then, I knew that this did not excuse the way he was. I would beg him not to fight so much, not to go out of his way to put himself into dangerous situations. But he never paid any attention.

Even if he had listened to me, however, there came a point where he simply was unable to turn back the clock. Stuart's reputation was such that kids – often much older than he – would pick fights with him just to get a name for themselves. I seldom saw the actual battles, but many was the time Stuart would tell me what had happened, and it was amazing how often events repeated themselves.

Some bloke, desperate to assert himself, would come up to my brother and make his intentions known. 'I'm going to have you later.'

Stuart's response was always the same: he would laugh

in his face. 'Let's go, son,' he'd tell him confidently, and rather than wait for the aggressor to come to him, he would pile in. The result was invariably the same: my brother seemed unstoppable, and after he had asserted his authority, he would be at once invigorated and disparaging about his opponent. 'Silly cunt,' he would say. 'He thought he was hard. Bet he doesn't feel so fucking hard now.'

And each time he won one of these encounters, as he almost always did, his confidence would be bolstered, and any possibility that there might have been of him living a more peaceful life seemed to be further from his grasp.

He was expelled from school for fighting and playing truant; a few weeks later he was expelled from a second school. Stuart didn't care one bit: he didn't want to be at school any more than they wanted him there. Back in Ireland, he had been involved in petty crime, and it had never really been frowned upon by the friends he hung around with. In fact, as was the case when he'd distributed those Fray Bentos meat pies around the neighbourhood, more often than not it led to him being treated like a hero. So I guess it was not surprising that he should become more involved with petty crime as he grew older. It started off small – shoplifting and the like – but then I suppose it always does. Before long, though, his misdemeanours started becoming more serious: driving cars without a licence, for example, and of course getting into all those fights. He was about sixteen the first time he got nicked for grievous bodily harm. I don't recall the details of the incident, but I do remember it was against somebody a lot older than himself. Soon the police started knocking on our door, wanting to know where Stuart was and what he had been up to. It was something we got used to.

And yet, despite all this, the other side to Stuart's character remained. When we were alone together, brother and sister, off the streets and away from all the bravado and the battling and the constant pressure to assert his authority and fight off the bullies, he was just Stuart – the kid who had looked after me all my life. His popularity was not limited to his little sister, either. He would always be joking and laughing, the life and soul of any party. 'Humour's important,' he would say. 'You've got to have a laugh, otherwise the world would be a very sad and lonely place.' If I was down, he would do his best to cheer me up, and I wasn't the only recipient of his good sense of humour: girls seemed to flock to my brother, attracted by his reputation, probably, but also by his easy charm and the twinkle in his eye. There was no doubt that Stuart Horgan was a catch, and he was more than happy to enjoy the company of the girls who hung around him.

The more popular he became, of course, the less he was around in the evenings when Mum went out to work and Dad was working away on a job; and as Sean also started going out increasingly often, so Graham would have more opportunities to abuse me. He could do whatever he liked to me, and he knew it.

Graham's need to keep me under his thumb led to him becoming physically violent towards me. I suppose he needed to make me believe that he would have no qualms about carrying out the dreadful threats he constantly delivered whenever the abuse occurred, and if that was his aim, it certainly worked. He would constantly hit me for no reason. One of his favourite little games involved a small pellet gun that we had in the house. It fired minuscule ball bearings and was intended just for target practice, little more than a toy really; predictably, however, *I* was Graham's target. He would load the gun with pellets, then approach me and, with a sadistic kind of smile, fire them against my clothes, stinging my poor skin and making little red marks appear on it that filled me with embarrassment as I did my best to cover them up.

His favourite way of physically abusing me, however, was to use wet washing from the washing machine. He would make me fetch a wet pair of jeans or a wet towel – whatever there happened to be on that particular day, but the heavier the better – then fiercely beat me with it. The wet material whipped against my skin with much more vigour than it would had it been dry, and each lash sent a shock of pain across my skin that hurt me as much as it appeared to give Graham satisfaction. Jeans were the worst – the wetness seemed to transform them into particularly brutal, painful weapons, and he would always choose to use these if they were available.

I was completely helpless. He was a monster who had total control. I hated him so much. I hated the life he was forcing me to live; I hated what he did to me; I hated the way he made me feel; I hated the way he made me look at other kids and wish I was them; I hated the way he made me wish that I could escape far away from him and all the things he knew he could do to me with impunity. Gradually I realised that I was having violent thoughts towards him. I used to hope with a real passion that something terrible would happen to him. Perhaps on the way to our house he would be beaten up so badly that he would be injured and no longer able to come and babysit. Perhaps God, to whom I still prayed nightly, would make him die for what he was doing. Perhaps he would get caught in the middle of abusing me and be punished in some violent and humiliating way. But he never was beaten up; God didn't make him die; and he was too clever ever to risk getting caught.

I honestly thought it would never end. I thought my life would be like this for ever. One day, however, he made a mistake.

I was in the kitchen with Graham. Dad was away on an extended job which offered overtime. Stuart and Sean were out with their friends, and Mum had left to go to work. The minute she was out of the house I had heard the strains of 'Almost Human' on the hi-fi, and had steeled myself against what I knew was about to happen. He had appeared at the door of my bedroom and, in a quiet voice, said the words that I so dreaded: 'We're going to play Jackie now, J-J.' He led me into my parents' room, locked the door behind us, and so it began.

I remember it being really, really horrible that night. I was told to remove my clothes as he stood over me, glaring and reminding me what would happen if I dared to refuse. He threw me down harshly on to the bed while he undid his trousers, slowly grinning as he forced himself upon me. It hurt just like it always did, but he was particularly brutal that night, and I whimpered with pain as he pleasured himself in his own sick way at my expense. It was as if he had to make doubly sure it was unbearable. It seemed to go on for ever.

'Please stop,' I cried after what felt like an age. 'Please stop, you're really hurting me. I think I'm bleeding. I don't like it.'

He looked at me, his face close and sneering, then withdrew. For a moment I felt a sense of relief, but I soon realised that it was misplaced as he grabbed me by my hand and then forced me down towards his genitals. I begged him not to make me, but he did not let up even though tears of distress were rolling down my face. The more I cried the longer he made me do it.

He wanted to do everything that night, and didn't seem satisfied until he had. And as was so often the case, when it was over he seemed even more aggressive than usual. He ordered me into the kitchen and the viciousness continued.

As he frequently did, Graham had been dominating me by withholding food – it was one of his ways of maintaining his grip. Sometimes he would starve me, other times he would let me have just a little taste of food so that I could imagine what it was like to have more, but then declare that tea was over. Sometimes, after I had played Jackie with him, he would let me eat; but not always. It depended on his mood.

He started screaming at me for something – I can't remember what. I knew he was on a mission that night, that this behaviour was a prelude to more violence or abuse, so I sat there quietly, looking down at the table and praying that whatever this scene turned into, it wouldn't be too brutal.

He was getting really cross with me now. He disappeared for a moment, then returned with a towel. I knew it would be wet – he always made sure it was before he beat me with it.

'Stand up,' he growled.

I stayed still.

'*Stand up!*' he repeated, taking a threatening step towards me.

Silently I pushed the chair back. As I did so, I glanced towards the kitchen door. Normally, if there was going to be some sort of violence, he would lock it in advance to make sure that nobody walked in on us from outside; but on this occasion, he seemed so wrapped up in his own anger with me that he had totally forgotten. I felt frightened: frightened of what he was about to do to me, of course, the pain he was about to inflict; but frightened too that someone would walk in. It didn't really occur to me that if that happened he would be exposed, caught red-handed. Instead, I thought that I would be caught doing something I shouldn't be doing. Being bad. I silently wished that he would lock the door so that at least I could be sure of keeping the beating to myself.

Graham stared at me with the flat look in his eyes that always announced his intention to start.

He was expert at flicking the towel wherever he wanted it to go, and instantly I felt the wet fabric lash against the skin of my face and hands. As they always did, hot tears of shame and agony welled in my eyes, but I knew it was better to stand there and take it rather than struggle. The sooner he finished, the sooner it would be over.

How long it went on for, I'm not quite sure; I just shut

my eyes and let it happen. Suddenly, though, there was a click, and the door opened.

I felt a sudden rush of cold fear surge through my veins. I was going to be in such bad trouble. Tentatively I opened my eyes to see who it was; and I will never forget the scene that greeted me as I did so.

It was Stuart. Unusually, he had come back early, and he stood in the doorframe with a look of blank incomprehension on his face as he took it all in. Graham had frozen like a statue, his arm half-raised to administer another whip of the towel. Gently, as though in slow motion, he let it drop. 'All right, Stuart?' he said, a tense tremor in his voice.

For a moment Stuart didn't respond; but as he stood there in silence I watched his face change from being stunned to displaying ferocious anger as it became clear to him what was going on.

'What the fuck are you doing?' he whispered.

Stuart wasn't a big person, but he suddenly emanated an aura of pent-up aggression that would have made even the toughest guy think twice about taking him on. Graham was no tough guy. He was a coward, someone happy to prey on people weaker than himself.

'It's all right, I was just mucking about.'

I had never seen anybody foaming at the mouth, but all of a sudden that was what Stuart started to do: little bubbles of saliva started to appear at the edge of his lips.

Graham must have seen it too, seen how angry he was becoming, because he started gabbling incoherently. 'She was being bad, wasn't she? A right pain to look after tonight – driving me mad. I was just mucking about. It was just a game, really.'

But it was as if Stuart couldn't hear him. He stepped forward without closing the door behind him, and as he moved towards Graham, my abuser visibly shrank back. Stuart bore down on him and Graham walked back towards the stairs as I watched in a kind of fascinated, thrilled horror.

The first punch was so quick that I didn't even see his hand; but for all his quickness, it was heavy, brutal and landed right in the centre of Graham's face. He crumpled, his nose bloodied, and cowered to the floor.

'Don't, Stuart,' I called half-heartedly. I felt scared by the violence that I knew was about to happen, and even then I didn't relish the idea of it being done in my name; but I would be lying if I said there wasn't some sense of satisfaction that finally the one who had inflicted such misery on me was getting a taste of his own medicine. I couldn't help feeling that this was right; this was how it should be.

'Please,' I heard him say, his voice pathetic, but Stuart didn't even give him the chance to beg. He laid into him with all his might, a whirlwind of punches and kicks that knocked the wind and all the strength out of my abuser.

I stood there and watched, not quite able to believe that the person who had dominated and terrified me for so long could be so easily and instantly floored.

Stuart never let up. Blood and spittle flew in the air, and whimpers came from Graham's mouth, he started pleading to Stuart, crying like a baby.

'Please, Stuart, leave me alone . . . Don't hit me again, Stuart . . . I was only messing around, Stuart. Honest I was . . .'

He was a different person from the one I knew. Suddenly he was the victim.

My brother grabbed him by the scruff of the neck with one hand and pulled him firmly and roughly off the floor. When he spoke, his voice was menacing: it demanded to be taken seriously. He raised his clenched fist in front of Stuart's face.

'If you ever . . .' *Punch.* '. . . ever . . .' *Punch.* '. . . ever . . .' *Punch.* '. . . touch my sister again, I swear I'll fucking well kill you.'

The threat hung in the air as Stuart stared implacably down at Graham, who returned that look with such fear in his eyes.

'Do you understand?' Stuart hissed.

No reply.

'*Do you understand?*' Another punch.

'Yeah, Stuart. I understand,' he said, clutching his bloodied face, his eyes full of fear.

My brother looked dubiously at him, and there was a dreadful silence as he decided whether he had punished Graham enough. Clearly, however, he decided not. He grabbed him by his hair, then pulled him like a rag doll across the room. Graham shrieked with pain, but Stuart was deaf to it: he started striking him all over again with his fists, relentlessly, repeatedly. Blood was everywhere, and I dared not say anything as I watched the scene that was unfolding before my eyes.

'You're vermin,' Stuart shouted. 'Fucking vermin!' And he let fly another flurry of punches as he shouted all manner of abuse at his victim.

When he had finished, and Graham was lying on the floor, clutching himself and rolling in agony, my brother approached me. I had seen him in fights before, of course, but I had never seen the look in his eyes that I now saw. It frightened even me, and it showed no sign of softening as he came in my direction.

'If he ever hits you again,' he said, out of breath as a result of his brutal exertions, 'you tell me. Do you understand?'

'Yes, Stu,' I said quietly.

'If you don't tell me,' he insisted, his voice sounding slightly out of control now, '*I'll* hit *you*. Got it?'

'Yes, Stu.'

'Good.' He turned round, gave Graham one final kick in the guts for good measure, then turned back to me. Stretching out his arms, he gestured at me to come to him. I needed no persuading. I ran into his arms, ignoring the fact that he had Graham's blood on his hands, and wept with blessed relief as he hugged me tightly.

'I love you, Jayne,' he said, his voice slightly grizzled.

'I love you too, Stu,' I wept. And it was true. In that moment, I loved my brother more than anyone else in the whole world. It was as though he was my angel, there finally to deliver me from Graham's never-ending viciousness. He held me tight, and just then I became closer than I had ever been to telling him the truth, to revealing the full extent of Graham's wickedness. But I didn't dare – for all the usual reasons, of course, but also because I honestly thought my brother would kill him if he found out what had really been going on. Still, I looked down at Graham, lying in a crumpled, bloodied heap on the floor, and I knew that he would think very, very hard before touching me again.

After a minute or two, Stuart released me from his arms. 'I'm not going out again tonight,' he reassured me, and I smiled gratefully at him. 'I'm going to call my mates – they can come round here for once.'

He looked down at Graham, who was just beginning to

scrape himself up from the floor. 'So you don't need to babysit any more tonight,' he spat. 'Fuck off.'

Graham staggered to his feet, looked from one of us to the other, then attempted to dust himself down and regain some of his dignity. 'Yeah,' he said, 'well, I've got friends to go and see tonight anyway.'

It was obviously a lie, something to make himself sound less pathetic, but Stuart let it pass. 'Fuck off out of it then,' he said shortly.

As I watched Graham turn and walk out of the door, I was barely able to contain my excitement. The horror of that evening's abuse seemed to fall from me, and I felt safe and secure in my own home for the first time in I don't know how long.

Soon Stuart's friends came round. They were friendly and boisterous, and although they paid me little attention as they spent the evening watching Bruce Lee videos, I was glad that they were there. Occasionally Stuart would catch my eye, and something unspoken would pass between us before he turned his attention back to his friends.

For myself, I went to bed. My covers that night provided me comfort rather than scant protection, and I lay there safe in the knowledge that nobody would come striding into my room demanding obscene favours of me that I did not want to give. Making me do the most terrible things.

And that night, for the first time in years, I slept like a child.

I was eleven years old.

# 6
## *The Scars*

For years I had been like a seedling, unable to grow because the sun was being blocked out by some big and sinister tree. The child inside me that should have been so happy and carefree was stunted and cowering in the darkness. Now, though, the tree had been chopped down, and it was as if the shadows had been chased away and I could feel the warm rays on my face once again. The air around me was no longer dirty, but clean.

Graham was still babysitting when my parents went out to work – I had not told anyone about the abuse, and Stuart had kept the facts about what had happened from my parents – but I knew that, after my brother's intervention, he would never dare touch me in that way again, even if he remained unpleasant, aggressive and bullying. Harsh words, though, I could deal with. Even though I was only little, I now realised that I had been carrying around with me a burden that no child should have to bear; now, however, that burden had been lifted from me and I could start living the life that had been so cruelly interrupted when we left Northern Ireland.

Of course, the scars of his abuse would never leave me; even now, after all the tumultuous, terrible events that were to follow in my life, I still wear them. I would wake up in the night, my sleep riddled with nightmares, half-expecting him to be there. And I still suspected, deep down, that it was all my fault in any case: you don't spend all that time as a child thinking that you are dirty and naughty and allow it simply to fall away from you. I hated Graham more and more, and my sense of desperation and injustice at what had happened did not leave me. But at least now I could look to the future with more confidence, safe in the knowledge that the abuse had finally stopped for good.

I started to blossom. The fact that he no longer dared to interfere with me gave me a confidence I did not previously know I had; and the fact that I no longer needed to wet the bed to keep him away – or have him urinate on my bedclothes – meant that I had a better chance of making friends, both at school and at home. In the blinking of an eye, my life appeared to have changed. My best friend was still Pepper the dog, my secret confidante, but I started to have real friends too. Melanie was one. She was such a lovely person, and we grew close enough for me to be able to tell her certain things – not about Graham, but I told her about how I felt when the kids at school picked on me, and it was good to have somebody outside the family to share these things with. Being friends with Melanie also gave me an insight into the way other families were. Sometimes I would go home with her at lunch breaks. She seemed to have everything a child could want, and her mum would cook a nice hot meal for us and give us glasses of orange juice. It was bliss.

There were lots of times, as I embarked upon my teenage years, that I longed to tell Stuart about the abuse I had suffered at Graham's hand; many was the time I found myself on the verge of discussing that dark chapter in my life with the one person in the world to whom I was closest. But while my love for Stuart was unqualified, I was not blind to his faults. I had witnessed the punishment he had meted out to Graham when he thought he was merely beating me with a wet towel; the anger that would be inspired in my brother if he knew the full extent of my maltreatment did not bear thinking about. I honestly believed my brother would have killed Graham; and while I would not have mourned his death, I did not want Stuart to have that blood on his hands.

There had been enough suffering because of Graham; I had no wish for there to be any more.

And so I kept quiet, just as I always had done. The nauseating secret that Graham and I shared remained just that: a secret. Shameful. Sickening. Horrifying. But a secret nevertheless. As I grew older, and it became less necessary for us to have a babysitter, Graham's physical presence in our lives waned. We would see him now and then, and if I found myself alone with him he would be as unpleasant to me as ever he was; but verbal abuse I could deal with, as long as he kept his hands off me. Sometimes, in my darkest dreams, I would have visions of him in my room, in my bed; sometimes I would still cry and feel ashamed by what I had done. But as it had when I was a very little girl, the rising of the sun chased away the shadows in my mind.

As time passed, and Graham's abuse became for me a memory rather than an ever-present reality, so I knew the chances of him ever answering for his crimes became more distant. The longer I left it, the less likely it was that anyone would believe what I had to say.

And so the harrowing events of my childhood years were being swept under the carpet; and in a way I suppose I was happy for that to be the case. Perhaps now I could forget the past and look to the future; a future unblemished by the violence that had surrounded me as a child.

It was a simple wish. But it was not to be.

It is said that paedophiles see it as their tragedy that the objects of their affection must inevitably grow up. It is this that spurs them on to find new children to prey upon, new childhoods to steal and lives to ruin. Whether Graham had found a new victim, I couldn't say; but I was certainly surprised when I learned that he was to be married.

There was another surprise in store for me too. When I was thirteen, my parents announced that we were moving house again. We were to make our new home in London, where Mum and Dad were going to take over the running of a pub. Just as I had found moving from Northern Ireland traumatic, now that Graham was gone and I was really settling into my life with my friends, I didn't want to move again; and I especially didn't want to move to London. It sounded like such a big, scary, difficult place to me, and we were to take up residence in one of the roughest parts of town. Mum and Dad's pub was a real East End boozer, located on the Isle of Dogs; there was nothing quiet or refined about it, and the moment I set eyes on it I knew I didn't want to be there. I wanted to be back home – I wanted to be anywhere but here. I would overhear Mum and Dad's horror stories of what life in London was like – tales of junkies and guns – and I couldn't understand why anyone would want to put themselves into that kind of environment. Worst of all, Stuart was not going to come with us. He had met someone, a lovely girl by the name of Vicky, and they were to stay in my parents' house while we made the move to London. I cried and I cried when I learned what was to happen, but my tears were in vain: this decision was not mine to make.

It was harsh moving to another school. I was the new kid

on the block, and for the first few weeks the other children were less than welcoming. I was desperate to make friends, and on one of my first days I latched on to this extremely good-looking girl. I followed her to the toilets so that we could smoke a cigarette together; when we were there, she brought out a small canister of lighter fluid. I watched in horror as she put it to her nose and sniffed deeply, inhaling the solvents deep into her lungs

I craved acceptance, so I watched her sniffing the lighter fluid as though I had no problem with it, but inside I was shocked by what I saw. It was my first encounter with drugs; it was not to be my last.

Mum and Dad's pub was big, with a public bar, a saloon bar and an off-licence. The clientele were predominantly bikers, and because they were the primary source of income, my parents went out of their way to welcome them, playing noisy, aggressive heavy-metal music over the pub speakers and doing whatever they could to make their pub the one that all the bikers wanted to come to. They were a rough, rowdy lot: they looked dangerous, but not nearly as dangerous as they actually were. On more than one occasion I was to witness scenes that should never have happened, let alone be viewed by a teenage girl.

There was a regular customer who went by the name of Micky Mars Bar. He wasn't a biker: unlike most of the pub's regulars, he was a quiet, placid, understated bloke who kept himself to himself, and never caused any trouble. One day, though, some kind of conflict blew up. Two of the bikers who were often in the pub – one black, one white, both of them junkies – got involved in a disagreement of some sort with Micky Mars Bar. The argument spilled out on to the street, and I watched from inside, through the protection of a window.

What I saw turned my stomach.

As the argument escalated, an axe appeared as if from nowhere; one of the bikers raised his arm and slammed it squarely into the side of Micky's face. It was like a horror movie – the whole of one side of his face seemed to flop away, and blood was everywhere. He started screaming, clearly in a blind panic as he desperately tried to hold his wounded face together; and the crowd that had gathered to watch the fight melted instantly away. An ambulance was called, and Micky was taken to hospital; not long afterwards, the police arrived to take witness statements, but nobody was willing to talk. It was that kind of place.

On another occasion, I was rather closer to the action. When I was a bit older, I used to help out behind the bar. I was underage, of course, but nobody really thought anything of it. It was just an ordinary night in the pub; suddenly, though, I heard my dad shouting at the top of his voice.

*'Jayne! Move out of the way!'*

Before I knew what was happening, he had put his arms

around me, tugged me away from where I was standing and hurled me under the serving hatch.

The bullet missed me by a matter of inches.

Some guy had walked into the pub with a shotgun, then quietly and calmly taken aim at one of the customers. He hadn't intended to target me; I just happened to be in the way. For years after that, there were two bullet holes in the wood to the side of the serving hatch, and they became something of an attraction – a reminder of the time a gun had been discharged in this pub. The clientele was such that, rather than scaring people away, this made it a more attractive place for them to come and do their drinking and brawling. For myself, I learned a valuable lesson: it's not the ones who brag and show off that you need to be careful of. Far more dangerous are the criminals who keep their own counsel but suddenly explode in a shower of violence. As a young teenager, I soon learned who to avoid.

Abuse doesn't stop merely because the abuser has finished his work; and just as the scars on Micky Mars Bar's face no doubt never left him, so I continued to carry the psychological scars of what had happened to me. Graham may no longer have been present in my life in a physical sense any more, but I still carried with me the lack of self-worth that he had instilled in my mind from the first time I met him; and the images of my early childhood seemed so deeply ingrained on my consciousness that I was sure they would never leave me.

I had buried it all so deep inside, I had hoped it was gone for ever. But now I felt myself falling apart. Throughout my formative years, I had been told that I was a bitch and a liar; I knew that I was bad and dirty. I'd tried to act like a normal girl, like my friends, but those sorts of feelings are not easily shed, and as a teenager I had a terribly low opinion of myself. Superficially it might have looked as though I was gaining confidence; in truth it was a different matter. I thought I was worthless; I thought I was wicked; I thought I was ugly, on the outside as well as the inside. The demons that plagued me throughout the years of abuse had taken up residence in my head, and I was not yet mature enough to force them to leave. I felt I had the need to compensate for my ugliness and so, as I entered my adolescence, I came to be of the opinion that the shorter the skirt I wore, the tighter the top, the less people would suspect the truth about me, or the secret that I was carrying. I craved the attention; but I hated myself for seeking it. It became a vicious circle that slowly started to eat away at any self-esteem I might have had.

Although I spent hours on my appearance, however, my attitude towards intimacy was a stark contrast. I might have been dressing myself up in what I thought of as attractive, appealing clothes, but the idea of having sexual contact with anybody disgusted me after the grisly encounters I had endured with Graham; and if anyone so much as came physically near to my body, it felt wrong.

As time passed, however, a paranoia about the way I looked would become the least of the mental scars that I carried with me.

Bulimia nervosa is a well-known eating disorder to which individuals who have suffered traumatic events in their life such as child abuse are especially prone. It is a dangerous, scary mental condition, usually less to do with the food itself than the psychological factors that cause the disorder in the first place. I found myself gradually becoming more and more bulimic as the months passed. I would go without eating for days; then, when I could bear it no more, I would binge, eating far more than any ordinary person would eat at one sitting. When I had eaten everything I could get my hands on, however, I would be overcome with the need to purge myself of the food I had just consumed. There were two ways I would try to achieve this: by making myself sick, or by taking strong laxatives. Often I would go for days without eating, then buy myself a huge box of chocolates and scoff the lot – not just because I was particularly fond of chocolate, but because when I vomited it up the sweet taste that remained in my mouth gave me the illusion that I had been eating properly rather than being sick, and I would not feel quite so hungry. But these techniques were designed to rid myself of the food I had eaten so that it passed through my body without being digested. I had a horror of putting on any more weight. I didn't want people to think I was uglier than they already did. Standing in front of the mirror, I would be greeted by a picture of skin and bones, but that's not what I saw: I saw a grotesquely fat girl. I saw somebody who needed to be punished. I saw somebody who did not deserve to enjoy life. Someone bad.

My mum, of course, knew that something was wrong. I may have thought I was second best in her eyes, but I was her daughter and she could not stand by and watch me deteriorating without growing worried. She did everything she could to try and snap me out of my eating disorder. She tried every approach: cajoling me, getting angry, finally persuading me to go away and stay with my auntie and uncle in Southend. But there was nothing she could do. When you feel so dirty and worthless, both inside and out, you find you have a need to make yourself atone, in some way, for the wicked things that you have done, or for allowing them to be done to you. And in some twisted way it seems better to hate yourself, because then you're not surprised when other people hate you. At the same time, you are ashamed at what you are doing, so you hide your condition from everyone. Apart from the people closest to me, no one would have known what I was going through, because I went to such lengths to hide it.

The cycle of bingeing and purging was relentless. It was dangerous. It was demeaning. And each time it happened, I was constantly aware of one thing: Graham may have been out of my life, but the residue of his abuse continued to be a scar on my very existence. I was free of him in one sense; but in another I remained his victim. It sometimes felt like he would be with me for ever.

I left school at the age of fourteen and started working for my parents in the pub. Of course, to work behind the bar I needed to look eighteen, and as a result, dressing up in adult clothes became even more the norm for me. The skimpier the outfit and the more make-up I plastered on, the easier I found it to get along with the locals, who clearly had a predetermined idea of what a barmaid should look like; but it only served as more fuel to feed the fires of my insecurity. And the more insecure I felt, the more I tried to find ways to battle it.

One day, when I was working in the pub, my drink was spiked. It was only once I had finished it that the locals who had played this 'trick' on me told me that I had just taken a dose of speed. I had never done anything like that before, and it was not the sort of thing that I would ever have got involved with. But I was keen to appear grown up, to fit in, so I acted like it was cool and fun. My eyes were pinned open, I stayed up all night chatting, and it seemed that as a result of taking speed, I was a little bit more popular.

And it felt good.

I decided I would do it again. And again. So started a short period in my life when I experimented with drugs: speed, magic mushrooms, marijuana. I would normally do them in the solitude of my own room, by myself, revelling in the knowledge that, although I was alone, I was breaking the rules and it was fun.

Sometimes, though, I would get together with friends and smoke marijuana or do speed. Part of me thought that I only had friends because my parents owned a pub – I was far too insecure to think that they were spending time with me because they actually *liked* me – and so I would go out of my way to be the one who bought the drugs, sharing them out generously. It made me feel popular; it made me feel like people wanted to be with me; it made me feel like I belonged; it made me feel normal. We would sit on walls, smoking and laughing about silly things. Laughter, I think, was the thing we enjoyed the most. None of us had much of that in our lives.

Occasionally Stuart would come down to visit, and together we would snort speed through a rolled-up bank-note, then go walking for miles, talking non-stop. And the good thing about speed was it stopped you being hungry, so I didn't want to eat.

To me it was like a moment of understanding: all my life, I had tried so hard to be good, but it only ever made me feel bad. The blame for that I knew I could lay squarely at the door of my abuser, but at the time it didn't matter. I had discovered that being *bad* could make you feel *good*. Of course, I was ignoring the fact that I was smothered by paranoia and low self-esteem; I was ignoring the bulimia. I thought I was starting to have a good time, and I believed this could only be achieved by going off the rails.

Little by little, I started becoming the sort of person that I never wanted to be.

# 7

# *Running Away*

Despite all the insecurities that were raging inside me, I had started making friends with people of my own age. Most of them lived in nearby West Ham, and they were a mixed bunch: boys and girls, black and white. The more I had to work and spend time away from them, the more resentful I became. I didn't want to be working – I wanted to be going out, getting drunk and smoking with my friends. When I was little, I wanted to be a child, but that opportunity had been ripped from me; now I was a teenager, I wanted the chance to be one, but I couldn't. Not really.

One evening, when I was sixteen years old, I was working the bar as usual, dressed up in my regular outfit of short skirt, tight top and high-heeled shoes. No doubt I was chatting away with the customers – slowly but surely I had started to strike up, if not friendships then at least wary acquaintances with some of them – when suddenly the door opened and a familiar but shocking figure walked into the pub.

It was Graham.

I had not seen him for a long time. I knew that he had been married, and had heard that he and his wife were now divorced, which hardly came as a shock to me. An inscrutable smile on his face, he came and took a seat at the bar, while I found myself unable to concentrate because of the overwhelming feeling of nausea that suddenly rushed over me.

'Hello, J-J,' he said.

My tongue turned to jelly, and I couldn't reply. He looked me up and down – approvingly, I thought, as though he reckoned I had dressed up like this for him.

'Your mum and dad around?' he asked.

The familiar old feelings of fear, white-hot and tingly, ran through my veins as I walked to the back of the pub to call my parents.

Graham started chatting to the locals, I don't know what about, but more than once I saw them glance over at me as they were talking; I felt sure that whatever Graham was saying about me, it was unlikely to be nice. I started getting strange looks from people, and occasionally Graham would fix me with his familiar sneer, and I knew that the old power games were starting up again. If he could not control me sexually, he would have to control me psychologically. There was no way I could fight back. My instinct was to run, but I had nowhere to go.

Later that night, things went from bad to worse.

Graham came up to the first floor of the pub where we lived. He was all sweetness and light to my parents, of course. I hid up in my bedroom, as I could not bear to be in his presence or to hear the poison that was coming from his lips. I started preparing for bed, and all the old feelings of terror welled up in me; just as I had when I was a little girl, I decided that I would not undress when I got into bed, but would instead remain fully clothed, as though my skimpy skirt and top would form some sort of barrier of protection against him. I felt as if I was eleven years old again, knowing that somewhere in the house there was a real-life monster. I did not think he was here to rape me – not now, and not with my family in the house – but I knew with some kind of unspoken certainty that something was going to happen tonight.

Sure enough, before I was able to get into bed, he was there, framed in the doorway of my bedroom just like he used to be. There was a wildness in his eyes; an anger. I felt utter panic.

His lip curled up into a sneer. 'You're a slag,' he told me. 'You know that, don't you? A slag and a whore. Look at the state of you.'

'Get out,' I whispered, but he ignored me and stepped further into the room.

Before I knew what was happening, he attacked me. 'You're a stupid, stuck-up bitch,' he hissed, pushing me to the floor.

'Leave me alone!' I tried to stand up for myself, but I had barely spoken when he started to rain blows down on my head. I was too stunned, too terrified even to cry out. Why he wanted to do this to me I don't know, even now; but before I knew it, he had opened my bedroom window and forced me out of it, hanging me from the windowsill and threatening to let me fall to the ground.

'You're only good for being a prostitute now,' he told me.

'Please, don't drop me,' I wept, but he wasn't listening.

'Just a prostitute,' he repeated. 'Your family are disgusted with you, did you know that? The people in this pub have told me all about you tonight. How you hang out with those black people, giving them drinks, having sex with them and listening to their music. Becoming one of them.'

I couldn't reply to his horrible words; I simply begged him not to hurt me any more, to pull me back into the bedroom and leave me be. I honestly thought, though, that he had finally gone over the edge and in a fit of madness was going to let me fall with no thought for the consequences. When he deemed that I had suffered enough, however, he heaved me back in through the window, pushed me crying to the floor once again, and left.

I wept and shuddered and gasped for several minutes as I frantically tried to regain my composure. What had happened was so brutal, so out of the blue, that it had shocked me to my very core. I thought of telling people what he had done, but the old insecurities took me over. I knew I wouldn't be believed, and that he would smooth-talk his way out of it. I knew I could never hope for justice.

There seemed to be only one option for me now, one thing I could do to regain control of my own life. If I could not remove the bad things from my world I would have to remove myself.

I would have to run away.

It barely took me any time at all to reach the decision; and once the decision had been made, there was no point in waiting. I would do it the very next night.

I wrote a letter to my mum and dad. It was short but affectionate, telling them how much I loved them and would miss them. I said that I was sorry if I had ever disappointed them over the years, but that this was something that I had to do and maybe with me out of the way their lives would be easier. I did not mention Graham; I gave them no inkling about what had gone on.

And then I sat and waited.

It was about three in the morning, when all the house was quiet, that I left. Carrying two carrier bags containing handfuls of clothes and a toothbrush, and still wearing my skimpy clothes and high-heeled shoes – flat shoes and trousers might have been more sensible, but I thought that they were unattractive and unfeminine – I crept out of my bedroom and into the kitchen, holding my breath and praying that I wouldn't wake anyone. The whole of our living area was on the first floor above the pub, and the kitchen had a door that opened out – rather dangerously – on to a sloping roof. I tottered on to the treacherous roof, then along a wall that led away from the house.

Suddenly, I heard a voice. 'Jayne! What are you doing?'

I turned round sharply, almost falling as I did so, to see a man I recognised as one of the pub regulars.

'What you doing?' he repeated.

I felt ridiculous. 'I'm running away,' I whispered.

'But it's the middle of the night. Where are you going to go?'

I looked around me a little helplessly – it wasn't a question to which I had a satisfactory answer. 'Anywhere other than here,' I said finally.

'You're mad,' he told me.

'Yeah,' I replied, 'maybe I am. But don't tell anyone you've seen me. *Please*. I just want to get away for a bit.'

He shrugged as if to say 'Have it your own way', and walked on.

When I found myself on my own again, I began to feel afraid. Where *was* I going to go? I didn't have any money, and I didn't want to go anywhere that people would think of looking. As if on autopilot I made my way to some nearby blocks of flats. They were not high-rise, but short, squat old towers, loads of them, from where many of the pub's customers came. I knew that there were plenty of empty apartments around here, and that the place was a magnet for vagrants and squatters, so I figured that I would be able to find somewhere to stay for one night at least.

I hurried towards them. It was dark and eerie; people occasionally wandered past me, vacant looks in their eyes that suggested they were high on whatever their drug of choice was. I was scared of them, but they didn't notice me as I hurried into one of the blocks.

Any number of the flats in this particular block were inhabited by squatters, and I timidly poked my head around the doors of a few of them: what I saw did not encourage me to venture further in. They were dark and dingy; there were used needles on the floor that suggested to me that these places were very dangerous. I may have dabbled in recreational drugs in the past, but I had a real horror of needles: I decided not to stay in the flats with the squatters, so instead I took up residence in the stairwell, huddling down on the cold concrete floor with nothing to keep me warm, counting the passing seconds as I waited for daybreak to come.

I felt cold, and alone. I felt vulnerable and unloved. I felt that I had hit rock bottom, shivering in that unknown, scary place. And yet I knew that nothing would persuade me to go back home.

Home, it seemed, was where horrors happened, and I wanted no more of them.

Dawn arrived. I had not slept, my limbs were aching and I wanted to get away from there. I hit the pavement and walked through the steely grey morning to East Ham; as soon as it was late enough, I called on my friends and told them that I had run away. They supported me, and I felt immediately bolstered by that support.

I knew I had to find myself somewhere to stay, so I went to the housing benefit office and filled in the forms that would allow me to find myself a bedsit – a poky little place, cramped and sparsely furnished, but it was my own space and that felt good. Never mind that I was barely old enough, and certainly not in the right state of mind, to be living on my own. I could have my friends over – although having black people in the bedsit did not go down well with the landlord – and on the outside I felt like I was starting to have a life again. The landlord was a friend of one of the regular customers in the pub, so through him word that I was safe filtered back to my parents; I suppose it was a relief for them to know that, and they made the decision that it was best to leave me alone during this period. But at the time I had no idea that they were keeping a discreet eye on me; I thought they hated me, and that for all they knew I was dead. I was wallowing in self-pity.

The eating disorder that had plagued me for the past couple of years had not gone away; now that I was left to my own devices, it grew worse. I could go for longer and longer stretches without eating; when I did finally binge, my food would come from tins and would not stay in my system long enough to provide me with nourishment even if they contained any. I grew from thin to thinner, unaware of the damage I was doing to my body.

In addition, and unbeknown to me, my rent wasn't being paid – probably I had filled out the forms incorrectly at the benefit office – and so my landlord started to take against me and it became clear that I would have to leave. Fortunately I was still in contact with a couple of the customers at the pub, bikers with long hair and hippy ways, who put me up before finding me a place to stay at the home of a friend of theirs, who was looking for a full-time nanny for her children. I stayed there for several weeks, but frankly the house was a state, the children were out of control, and my health was deteriorating rapidly. I wanted to find somewhere else to stay; little did I know that my next residence would be a hospital room.

My malnutrition and bulimia had caught up with me. I guess you can't go on abusing and neglecting your body for that long without there being some kind of fallout. I was lucky, I think, that my path took me to a hospital bed and not on to the streets. I was painfully thin and under-nourished, with a stomach infection causing anxious doctors and nurses to be by my bedside day and night. They rehydrated me, pumped me full of antibiotics and other drugs, and did their best to get some sort of nourishment into me. I was in a complete state – my body had shut down.

Word got out of my plight, and eventually made its way back to a few of the customers at the pub, who told my mum and dad that I was lying in a London hospital. My mum turned up immediately. Even though it was me that had run away from home, I was glad to see her. I think she must have been deeply shocked to see my condition: it was an emotional moment, both of us in tears at having to be reunited in this way. 'Jayne, love,' she said, 'you've got to come back home.' And I had to admit that she was right: home was where I needed to be – at least until I had recovered – and I was welcomed back into the pub.

It didn't take me long to realise, however, that I could not stay there for long. Nothing had changed: since Graham's sudden reappearance, being at home held too many bad memories for me, and I knew I would have to leave again soon. This time, however, I was better prepared.

A friend of mine had set me up with an interview for a hostel run by an organisation called the Kipper Project, designed to stop young people having to live on the street. I went to the interview and, to my astonishment, was offered a place in their hostel opposite Mile End underground station. I couldn't believe my luck – for once something was going right. I didn't tell my parents, as I wasn't sure what their reaction would be; rather than slip out of the house in the small hours of the morning as I did before, however, I was a bit more savvy. They had booked to go on holiday to Spain, leaving my auntie and uncle to look after the pub. I waited until they were safely abroad, and then I left.

It was two days before my seventeenth birthday. The Kipper Project couldn't let me in until I was actually seventeen, so I would have to make do for forty-eight hours until my place became available. I knew that I could have headed into the West End and stayed a couple of nights at Centrepoint, where they gave shelter to homeless people; but equally I knew that that was where all the real down-and-outs and the junkies ended up, and I was scared to put myself among them. I decided to stay in the area that I knew.

Near the hostel there was a block of flats – nicer than the ones I had headed to when I ran away for the first time, but still hardly a luxurious spot. I could think of no other option, however, so much as I had the first time round, I took up residence in the stairwell of that block of flats. I decided I would stay halfway up – that way, if I ran into trouble from anyone coming at me from below, I could escape up the stairs; trouble from above and I could escape down. I huddled up, and waited for my seventeenth birthday to arrive.

It was bitterly cold; and as night fell it only became colder. I tramped around the streets for a while in an attempt to keep my body temperature up, but soon my legs started to ache – whether because I had been walking so much or because of the temperature, I don't know. So I returned to the block of flats and huddled down in the corner of the stairwell. By midnight it was so cold that I couldn't feel my feet. I had no blankets, and no money. I knew I should probably continue walking around to keep my circulation going, but the muscles in my legs ached too, so I stayed put on that stone stairwell as the seconds ticked by, excruciatingly slowly. Those two days seemed like a year, and I had plenty of time to reflect on my situation. I thought back over everything I had experienced. I remembered the throbbing sounds of 'Almost Human'; I pictured Graham standing in the doorframe of my room saying, 'It's time to play Jackie now, J-J.' And I knew, deep down, that if it hadn't been for him and everything he had done to my body and my mind, I would not be here now. But I also knew that, despite my being on the edge of hypothermia, this was better than having him anywhere near me.

I shivered, and waited. And waited. And waited.

Finally the day of my seventeenth birthday arrived. With a great deal of effort I stumbled to the hostel that was just round the corner and banged feebly on the door.

I was ready to be given a new beginning.

# 8

# New Beginnings and Old Wounds

The hostel was a huge house divided into a number of small, self-contained rooms. I had a lock on my door, and my own shower cubicle, a bed and a fridge; elsewhere there was a washing machine and a tumble dryer. Now that I had a permanent residence I was allowed to sign on, so I had a small income, a portion of which was put aside by the hostel people for when I finally moved into my own place. The residents would share the chores, so the hostel was always neat and tidy, and everyone was around the same age as I was, so I immediately started to feel, there amid the disenfranchised youngsters, who all had their stories to tell, that I belonged.

There were people from all walks of life. Some of them were friendly; many were scary, with dark sides to their characters. There was a girl who was so fiery and aggressive that I was scared even to look at her. She was covered in piercings and carried around with her the kind of attitude that made you pray she didn't take anything you said or did the wrong way.

But for all the strange characters, there were kind ones as well. I became particularly friendly with one young man who was very skinny with dark hair and a huge number of big red spots all over his face. His eyes always looked shadowy, and he would stare at people in a peculiar way as he shambled around the hostel. The first time I met him I could see he was a very unhappy person, and it didn't take long to discover that he was a helpless junkie. He was always hanging around in the corridors asking me – or anyone who passed him – if I had any drugs. Failing that, he would ask, with a hint of despair in his voice, whether I had any money. More often than not I didn't; even if I did I wouldn't have given him any. Instead I would offer him some food, and although that was not what he was after, he seemed grateful enough for it. Even though I sometimes helped him out, I remained scared of him, always feeling slightly on edge if he was around. There was something about him – an aura, if you like – that suggested he could explode at any minute, and you got the idea you didn't want to be there when that happened.

I also made friends with a girl who had herself had a traumatic family upbringing. We would talk long into the night about our experiences. Generally speaking, though, I kept myself to myself, vowing never to go back to the former life that I found so difficult for so many reasons.

By this time, neither of my brothers was living with

Mum and Dad. Stuart was in Buckinghamshire, but I did not even call him, so keen was I to make a clean break from my past; and I had never been that close to Sean, so he and I fell largely out of contact. I should have known, however, that of all people, Stuart would not have let me slip out from under the protective wing of his care for long. Mum must have got in touch with him to say that I had left home again; he came down to the pub and started making discreet enquiries as to my whereabouts among those regulars who knew me. One lead led to another, and soon enough he tracked me down.

It was such a relief to me, the day he got in touch. He sounded so cheerful, so infectiously happy, that it raised my spirits immeasurably. He was living with his long-term girlfriend, Vicky, at the time, in High Wycombe, and he insisted that I come and stay with them for a couple of days. I accepted gratefully, and when I went to visit, he spoiled me rotten, taking me out, treating me, generally making sure that I had as nice a time as possible. And of course, he showered me with questions. Was I all right? Was I having any problems? Why did I leave the pub? Was it anything to do with Graham suddenly being back on the scene? Was he giving me grief?

I listened to his anxious questions, smiled, and reassured my concerned brother. 'I'm fine,' I told him. 'The only reason I left was because I'd had enough of living in a pub.'

Stuart eyed me suspiciously while I did my best not to let my true emotions show on my face.

'You're not in touch with Mum and Dad, or Mandy, or Sean?'

I shook my head.

'Look, Jayne,' he said finally, 'I've got an idea.'

'What is it, Stu?'

'Why don't you come and live with us?'

I fell silent. Stuart's face was beaming with enthusiasm for his idea.

'No, Stuart,' I said finally.

'Why not?' he asked, sweeping an arm around him to indicate that there was plenty of space. 'We've got loads of room. Why do you have to stay in that hostel? We'll look after you . . .'

I gently put my hand on his. 'No, Stuart,' I said as kindly as I could. 'Please don't worry about me. I'm fine. I need to learn to stand on my own two feet.'

It was a precious few days that I spent with him; but the time soon came for me to return to the hostel in Mile End; I did so with a heavy heart, but knowing it was the right thing to do. Even though we were separated by the miles, however, I felt as close to Stuart then as I ever had done, and we kept in regular contact from that moment on.

★

I became a new person living in the hostel. With the help of the staff there, I grew in confidence, and I began to master my eating disorder. Gradually I started to take control of my own life, and though the memories of Graham's abuse were still buried deep inside me, I vowed that they were not going to blight my life for ever. I was determined to move on.

There were many psychological obstacles I needed to sort out in order to do this, but perhaps the most difficult was my hatred of physical intimacy. After everything Graham had done, I could not bring myself to consider being with a man again; I could not even begin to imagine a scenario in which sex would be anything other than dirty, humiliating and traumatic. Sometimes, though, things happen when you least expect them, and now that I was away from home and meeting new people, I started trying to come to terms with these issues in my head.

My first boyfriend, David, was very mature for his age. He was a friend to start off with, and was very caring towards me at a time when I thought nobody else cared at all. Unlike a lot of the people who surrounded me, he didn't take drugs and didn't drink – he appeared to be a good influence, and I found myself wanting to be with him more and more. The first time we slept together was a turning point in my life. Of course I could not fully put my memories of Graham out of my mind, but it felt natural and intimate, as though it was the right thing to do; something normal between two affectionate people. I liked the way he made me feel, the security he gave me; I found that I needed to see him more and more.

It is easy, however, to mistake dependency for love, and looking back now I know that this was what I was doing. I wanted a little family of my own more than anything else, and for the first time I was in a position to achieve this. I even managed to ignore the fact that I was beginning to find sex difficult again – it kept reminding me of everything that had happened as a child. I could never bring myself to tell my boyfriend anything about how I felt, because I was afraid to appear messed up and sick.

What was more, I had an overpowering wish to have a baby.

I didn't tell David when I stopped taking the pill. In my confusion I hardly thought it was important. It didn't matter about him: I could look after a baby, even if he didn't want to.

I was overjoyed the day I found out I was pregnant. I realised that this was all I ever really wanted. I remembered the times I used to play with my dolls in my bedroom, creating an imaginary happy family in the midst of all the horror; I remembered how it had made me feel. Safe. Secure. Needed, in some childish kind of way. But now I didn't need dolls any more. I was going to have the real thing, and the love and excitement I felt for the baby growing inside me was palpable.

Unfortunately, David didn't feel the same way about the forthcoming arrival. He was understandably dumbfounded.

'I'm not ready for this,' he told me, shock in his voice.

It wasn't what I wanted to hear, but I tried to stop the disappointment from showing in my face.

'You can go, if you want,' I told him. 'I'll look after the baby. It'll be OK.'

To his credit, David stayed around, but the sudden strain on our relationship was enormous. He was too young for a fatherhood that I had forced upon him, and I started to become obsessed with the possibility that he might leave me. I think I knew at the time that I was only clinging on to him because what he offered was better than what I had at home, now Graham was hanging around again, that he could have been replaced by anyone who was willing to show me a bit of affection; but nevertheless I became manically possessive as the pregnancy progressed.

The key workers at the hostel were less than keen on my decision to have a baby. I don't blame them – I was very emotional at the time, always dissolving into floods of tears for no apparent reason. I would run out of my room with tears streaming down my face; someone would ask me why I was crying and I would yell at them that I didn't want to talk, then sprint back into my room. Despite the fact that leaving home was my choice, I think I was traumatised by the loss of my family, and was finding it very difficult to get used to.

The key workers knew of my background, of course; they knew that I had run away. More than once a concerned worker would take me to one side, hold me by the hand and say, 'Jayne, I think you're having this baby for the wrong reason. I think you're having this baby because you've got no other family, because you're lonely.'

'You're wrong,' I would tell them flatly. I was thrilled because at long last I would have somebody to care for and who would care back, a family of my very own. When they understood that I was serious, they were fantastic: they supported me brilliantly, and they put all their efforts into helping me find my first flat. And while the hostel had been a life-saver for me, I was excited to know that on my eighteenth birthday, heavily pregnant, I would move into my first little place in East Ham.

David was not living with me, nor was he planning to, but I was looking forward to him helping me move and settle in; perhaps he would even give me a small birthday present. We would be together in my own place, grown-ups finally. Days before I moved, I pictured the scene in my mind, and I felt a little thrill every time I did so.

The reality of my eighteenth birthday was quite different. I moved in by myself, and it was at that moment I realised the truth about our relationship. I fought back the tears, but I knew in my heart that, even though David had said he would stick around, I had to prepare myself for the fact that this relationship was not going to be everything I had hoped it might be. My possessiveness became too much for him to handle, and he left soon afterwards.

My baby was born, a healthy little girl who I named Emma. I doted on her and cared for her, revelling in motherhood and thanking God that I had been blessed with such a beautiful and happy child. The prospect of raising a child without any support, however, seemed scarier than it had before. As a result, I fell into the arms of the next man who came along. His name was John, and I thought he was in love with me. I was soon to find out how wrong I was – especially when the violence started. It began as bullying, but then I suppose it always does.

I did my best to shrug it off. Perhaps I should have realised from my past experiences, however, that when you allow someone to be aggressive towards you once, they take it as a sign that they can continue. He would pull my hair and slap me; more often he would terror-ise me with threats and harsh words. Our relationship deteriorated to the point where I would be regularly subjected to his petty bullying. It is true that I had become increasingly possessive about him, but he reciprocated that possessiveness tenfold.

One day he walked into the flat and immediately looked me up and down. 'What do you think you're doing?' he asked.

I shrugged, a bit confused. 'What do you mean?' I asked.

He looked at my legs. 'Where are your tights?'

'I'm not wearing any,' I replied quietly.

He strode over to me and poked me hard. 'Put your tights on,' he said in an aggressive whisper.

'But I don't want to wear tights.'

He slapped me really hard, and I shouted out in pain as he went to the bedroom, coming back with a pair of thick tights. 'Put them on,' he instructed as he shoved them sharply into my stomach. 'Now! And don't ever go round without them again. You look like a tart.'

I meekly did as I was told, just to avoid another bout of his sudden violence. But no matter what I did, the peace didn't last for long. I always did or said something that made him get mad with me.

One day I was invited round to some friends' house. 'Will you look after Emma?' I asked John.

'Why should I?' he asked. 'She's not my kid.' But I pleaded with him, and finally, reluctantly, he relented.

'All right,' he told me, but I could tell from his tone of voice that he wasn't very happy to be relegated to the position of babysitter.

I decided to go nevertheless. 'I won't be back late,' I promised.

It was a typical girly, gossipy evening. My friends knew the problems I had been having with John, and when I told them he hadn't been too happy about looking after Emma, one of them made a joke. 'He'll probably beat you up again for having a bit of freedom,' she said.

My friends laughed, but I silently looked at the floor and they fell quiet. 'Sorry,' the girl quickly apologised. 'I was only joking.' I knew that was true, but something about what she said had touched a nerve.

I kept my promise and was back home by nine o'clock. John seemed even crosser than he had been when I'd left.

'Do you want something to eat?' I asked, trying to diffuse the tension.

No answer.

'Can I get you a drink?'

'*No!*' he screamed. He stormed into the bedroom to go to bed. I followed him in.

The light was on in the bedroom, and I walked over to Emma's cot to check on her as I always did. I picked up the warm little bundle and held her gently in my arms.

'Turn the light off,' John said. I could hear anger in his voice.

'I'm only checking on her,' I replied. And then, in a moment of sudden bravado: 'Anyway, you turn it off.'

'You've got ten seconds to turn the fucking light off,' he told me, 'or else.'

*Or else*. I knew what that meant. Equally, however, I didn't honestly believe that he would grow violent over such a stupid little thing as turning the light off, and so to make my point I waited the full ten seconds before plunging the room into darkness.

I was still holding Emma when he hit me. Falling heavily to the ground, I felt him take the baby from my arms, before he carried on with the brutal beating, striking me viciously around my head and my face. When he had finished venting his anger, I crawled from the room and into the bathroom. Pulling myself up, I avoided looking at my bloodied face in the mirror, and my hands shook as I tried to wash the crimson stains from my skin. My lips and cheeks were numb with pain, but I did not examine myself too closely as I wanted to get back to Emma.

I staggered back into the bedroom, but when I got there I was overcome with a wave of dizziness. I fell to the floor, choking on my own blood.

And then John was there. 'Shit,' he whispered, sounding genuinely horrified at his handiwork. 'I'm so sorry, Jayne. Are you OK? Say something. Do you need to go to the hospital? I'll call a cab.'

He came with me that night, sitting outside the hospital room with my darling little girl while the doctors examined me. My teeth had been shattered, and as bits of tooth had become impacted in my gums, parts of my gum had to be extracted. I was given stitches to stem the bleeding on my face, and was unable to eat or drink for a week.

I explained to the hospital staff what had happened: they were supportive and sympathetic, and they urged me to report John to the police. But I didn't do that. It was more in my nature simply to accept what was happening to me, to assume that I was to blame in some way for the violence. And so I kept it all to myself.

For some time after that I submitted myself to his bullying. I would never be able to tell what had inspired it, but I learned to accept it just as I had learned to accept Graham's abuse. John never beat me again to the same extent as when I had ended up in hospital, but I always feared that he would turn on me, and sometimes fear is worse than the act itself. But still I tried to put it from my mind and get on with my life. To get on with looking after my baby daughter.

I don't believe that at the time John really wanted anything to do with Emma; but he was always looking for ways of hurting me, and not just physically. So it was that he started to make threats: threats of violence, certainly, but also threats that he would report me for being a bad mother, so that Emma would be taken away from me, and it was these that I feared more than anything. I became determined that no matter what he did to me, nobody would take my little girl away. I was still scared of him –

deeply scared – but through Emma, I had found a new kind of strength. I had a responsibility to my daughter, and I couldn't afford to be damaged goods any more. I was worth more than that and, more importantly, so was my daughter.

I went to the police and took out a court injunction against him. I knew that I had put an end to the cycle of violence, and I felt empowered at having done so. I like to think that my actions did something to help John too: after we split up I never heard of him ever hurting another woman, and by all accounts he has grown into a much nicer man.

I started working, taking on cleaning jobs that I could bring Emma along to. I also became involved with a voluntary organisation called Home-Start, a charity that exists to help families whose life has been affected by abuse, violence and alcohol. They gave me a twelve-week training programme, and I knew that because of my background I might well be able to help any parents or children who needed assistance. It was traumatic seeing other people having to deal with issues similar to those that had plagued my childhood; but it was cathartic too, another step I had to take towards healing the emotional wounds that Graham had inflicted upon me.

At the age of twenty-one, my life took another turn for the better when I met Simon. Instantly I could tell that he was different from other men that I had known: kind, considerate, fun, he was the sort of person with whom I could feel instantly at my ease. I kept my relationship with him secret from my daughter for a long time, because I was determined that her childhood would not involve a never-ending string of surrogate fathers: I would only introduce them to each other when and if I knew that Simon was somebody with whom I wanted to spend the rest of my life. That realisation soon arrived, and I began to feel as though I was putting even more distance between myself and the past. Our relationship was cemented with the arrival of our son, Luke, and we married soon after that.

The journey was not yet complete, however. I started having panic attacks, horrible moments of desperate anxiety when I felt as if my body had been dipped in freezing water before becoming insufferably warm and uncomfortable. I started counselling, and was diagnosed with post-traumatic stress disorder. When my drink was spiked with LSD in a club, I became convinced that this was some kind of cosmic punishment for my behaviour. All the old insecurities that I had felt as a child under Graham's control came flooding back, and I started being nervous about going out – a nervousness that I have not completely conquered to this day.

All the while, Simon stood by me. I told him of my past, and he held my hand as the counselling that I was undergoing forced me to confront my demons, to accept that I was not to blame for what had happened to me, to learn that I didn't deserve what Graham did. I started to have significant conversations with my parents again, which was, I think, an important moment.

And gradually my loathing for my abuser also changed. I still hated him, of course – that would never alter – but I started also to pity him.

How awful, I thought to myself, to be that person.

How awful to be a slave to so many twisted needs and desires.

And how awful to wake up in the morning and be struck by the realisation of who you are, and have to live with yourself after all the despicable things you have done.

Having left home I had cut off a large part of my contact with Mum and Dad. I was slowly trying to pick up the pieces of my shattered life and put them back together again. I needed to concentrate on my new family, I needed to become whole again.

Just as my life was becoming more stable, the same thing was happening to Stuart. He had been with his girlfriend, Vicky, for some time now, and for them, life seemed good. Stuart was enjoying his independence: he had regular work as a bricklayer and, while they were not rich, they had enough to pay the mortgage, have a nice car each and go on holidays abroad more regularly than most. Stuart was besotted with Vicky, and their affection for each other made them ambitious for their future together. For her part, Vicky appeared to know everything about Stuart: what he liked and didn't like, what hurt and what made him angry. She could handle him with a rare skill that made her the perfect partner for him. I adored her. Although she was similar in age to me, she had a kind of maturity that made you think she was older, and an elegance that I felt I could only strive towards for myself.

They had been going out for nearly ten years when Stuart finally proposed marriage. Everybody was so excited: they were the perfect couple, and after the shaky start Stuart had had in life, it was a relief to anyone who loved him that he now seemed intent on getting some kind of stability for himself. You only had to see them together to realise that Vicky was his true love, and the day they married was like a fairytale. She looked as beautiful as a princess; he was immaculately dressed in top hat and tails and I do not remember there being many dry eyes in the church that day.

They spent two weeks abroad on honeymoon, and when they came back Stuart could not stop talking about how wonderful it had been and how he hadn't wanted it to end. Both of them had work commitments, however – especially Stuart, who was running building sites by that time; but he threw himself into his work with gusto. It was pleasing to see Stuart doing his best to change himself for Vicky, as though finally he had a purpose in his life.

It was pleasing too to see the aggressive side of his character recede. One day, Stuart took Vicky out to dinner and asked her how she felt about them getting a pet. She agreed, and together they went to view a German shepherd puppy, whom they fell in love with the moment they saw him.

Insisting that the dog needed to be house-trained as early as possible, Stuart decreed that their new pet should spend his nights alone in the kitchen. Vicky agreed, so when they went to bed that night, the dog was shut firmly in the kitchen, where it proceeded to cry and scratch at the door. Stuart's tough attitude lasted for all of five minutes; after that he could not bear the sound of the animal's distress any more, so he apologised to his wife and went back down to the kitchen with a blanket. He slept there for three nights in a row, just so that the new addition to their family would not be lonely. When I heard what he had done, I could not help but remember the time, so many years previously, that Stuart had done a similar thing for me after I had cut my foot on the floor while being scared of monsters in our new house. After that, there was never a dog that was so well looked after. And while Stuart maintained his Jack-the-lad reputation, he seemed now to be happy to show the world the side to him that I always knew existed. The marriage had not produced any children, but I know Stuart hoped that would happen when the time was right.

I started going to visit Stuart and Vicky increasingly often during my early twenties, taking Emma with me. Together they would go out of their way to make sure that we had a good time, treating us and spoiling us as if we were their own kids. They were so impulsive that every day with them was different, and it was such a joy to be around them. Whenever we were there, the two of them would once more broach the subject of us coming to live with them, and I was sorely tempted to take them up on their offer. I would often think about it when I was alone in the faceless anonymity of London. Their house was such a happy place to be, and their desire for us to be around them so genuine. But I had Simon now, and my independence. Moreover, I did not like the idea of them having to support me and my daughter. I didn't want to be a burden, so I always refused their offer.

Maybe I shouldn't have turned them down. Maybe the presence of someone else in that house would have been a positive influence. Maybe, if I had been there with the brother who I loved so much, he would not have been tempted down the road he was finally to follow.

Or maybe that would have made no difference. Maybe he was what he was, and I was too blind to see it.

Maybe nothing could have halted what happened next.

# 9

## Confessions

They say that the child is father to the man. And while Stuart might have been demonstrating to Vicky and to the world at large that the caring, loving side to his personality was still very much alive, I suppose it was too much to hope that the other part of his character – the part that had learned to fight from the earliest age – would ever fully recede.

Stuart had a taste for the fast life. He loved to go out partying and clubbing, and Vicky enjoyed it too. While Vicky enjoyed a drink, however, she did not consume alcohol to the same extent as my brother. After all, Stuart had been brought up on a Northern Ireland estate where drinking alcohol to excess happened, and from his earliest teenage years he had been guzzling bottles of cheap cider with his friends. He had always liked drinking, but as the years passed his liking for booze had become more of a need, and the harder he partied, the stronger his alcohol habit became. At work he was pretty much expected to drink heavily with his workmates; it might have been acceptable had he not started binge drinking after work and during his precious weekends as well. Vicky, who previously had been his constant companion, started staying at home more regularly: I think she must have realised, as I did, that gradually the focus of Stuart's life was changing. Whereas before she had brought meaning to his life, now he was overcome with the conflict, chaos and confusion that only a dependency on alcohol can bring. I didn't blame her for not wanting to be part of it – she was too good for that kind of lifestyle.

Whether Stuart could ever have found his way back, I don't know; but soon he discovered something that made him feel even better than alcohol. This was the era of the Ecstasy pill, and once he had popped his first E, it made the possibility of turning back even more unlikely. He loved Ecstasy; it took hold of him and didn't let go. He loved the way it broke down barriers between people, making them come together in a haze of chemically induced harmony. He loved the way it heightened his emotions, and made him feel happy and loving towards everyone. People who were considered – by Stuart, at least – to be aggressive and unpleasant, the sort that you would go out of your way to avoid, were suddenly full of good cheer and friendliness. The change in people was unbelievable. Stuart used to describe it to me, his eyes shining with enthusiasm as he spoke. 'P.L.U.R., Jayne,' he would tell me. 'Peace, love, unity and respect. It's what it's all about.'

The love pill. It made everyone your friend. Perhaps that was what Stuart had craved all his life. Perhaps it seemed like his prayers had been answered. Perhaps that's why he never gave any thought to the side effects that it could have. Wherever he went out for the night, drink and drugs were readily available. He used to look forward to the weekend so much so that he could get, in his words, 'out of my fucking face'. Drunk and high, he felt on top of the world; but when you feel on top of the world, the only thing you can do is fall . . .

The after-effects of Stuart's spiralling drug habit became increasingly apparent. While the Ecstasy might have made him feel good when it was in his system, once he was sober he became riddled with paranoia and mood swings, and crushed by an insufferable depression. And, of course, the worse he felt, the more Ecstasy he needed to take that feeling away. He went from being Mr Likeable – always there with a joke and up for a good time – to Mr Changeable. You simply didn't know what kind of mood you were going to find him in next – nice Stuart or horrible Stuart. For Vicky, it must have been like living with Dr Jekyll and Mr Hyde.

When he couldn't put his hands on any Ecstasy, he found solace in alcohol. Instead of going home after work, he would go straight to the pub and the next day he would wake up feeling bad, and come lunchtime he would need more alcohol, so instead of going to a café as he would normally have done, he would start drinking again. He needed the alcohol just to get through the day.

I watched helplessly as it happened, my visits to the previously happy couple becoming less and less enjoyable. I knew Stuart well enough to realise that he would not listen to reason regarding his deteriorating behaviour, and it was with a dreadful sense of the inevitable that I stood by and watched his happy, perfect relationship with Vicky dissolve as he became addicted to booze and pills.

It didn't take Vicky long to decide that this was not what she wanted or deserved. She was a sensible woman, after all, and she didn't like the effect all this was having on Stuart any more than I did. It was obvious to everyone what Stuart was doing to their marriage; everyone except him. It made me unbearably sad the day she left, but it was not a surprise – most people would have done the same thing in the circumstances.

At first, Stuart seemed almost blasé about Vicky's departure: it meant he was a free agent again, and could do what he wanted, when he wanted, without having to explain his actions. Soon, though, it dawned on him what he had done: the buzz of the single life became boring, and the realisation of what he had lost became acute. In his moments of sobriety I would talk to him, and he would be open with me, a little boy once again. He told me how much he loved his wife, and how he wanted her back. He admitted that he was now drinking to drown out the pain of their separation, that there was not a single moment when he didn't want her to walk back into his life.

It saddened me so much to see my brother in this state. He knew what he had to do to win her back, and Vicky was willing to be worked on. She kept popping round to see how he was doing. But at the end of the day she didn't see a change in Stuart because there wasn't one. She started divorce proceedings. The moment he heard this, Stuart started to sink even deeper into the hole that was of his own making. He played it down in front of his friends, pretending that he wasn't bothered by Vicky's recent departure; but I knew different. Many was the time he told me how hurt he was, of the pain he felt, and I did my best to comfort him. It felt strange, me being the one to look after him, but it was the least I could do after all the times my brother had comforted me. But it was apparent that I could not say anything that could help him deal with the misery he was feeling: the only thing that helped was the bottle, and his drinking binges continued with grim regularity.

It was not just the drinking that was taking over his life; he started fighting too. Vicky had somehow managed to contain the angry young man that existed inside him, but now she was gone he surfaced once more. But I knew, without question, that the greatest anger Stuart felt was with himself.

For myself, I felt as though the tables were starting to turn. Whereas before it had always been Stuart who had protected and looked after me, now it was me who was listening to his problems, giving him advice and support.

After Vicky's departure, Stuart was distraught.

He would come and visit me in London fairly regularly, and when he'd had a drink, Stuart would start unloading to me.

'I still love Vicky, Jayne,' he would whisper sadly to me. 'I still *really* love her. I'm not happy and I'm turning into a monster.'

It was so horrible to hear him talking like that, as though he knew what was happening but was unable to stop it. I wanted the old Stuart back, the one who cared for people's feelings, the little boy who used to comfort me when I was sad. 'If you know you're turning into a monster, Stu,' I reasoned with him, 'why do you keep on doing what you're doing? Why can't you sort it out?'

'Oh, I don't know, Jayne,' he would say, deflated and demoralised, and would do his best to turn the conversation on to something else.

But things were clearly getting to him, and he would deal with this by drinking and taking drugs more often than he ever had done. I honestly believe his heart had been broken, but it was of his own making, and was no excuse for his behaviour.

Stuart had become a different person.

In his drunkenness and depression, he was someone I didn't recognise, unleashing his frustrations on everyone, even me, as I tried to make him see how much of a mess he was in. I begged him to get help for his drinking: 'At least try and get it under control, Stu. It'll help you think more clearly about things.'

My advice fell on deaf ears. All he could think about was Vicky. 'I want my wife back,' he told me.

But she wasn't coming back. Vicky was in a new relationship, and when Stuart heard about it he hit rock bottom. Alcohol and aggression had taken him over; his house and car were repossessed and he was declared bankrupt.

Around this time, he started to stalk one of his ex-girlfriends, someone he'd started seeing after Vicky left. He began hanging round her house and posting threatening letters through her door. I begged him to stop this behaviour, but he was full of urges and emotions that he could not control, and eventually an injunction was taken out against him. Stuart was not the sort of person to take much notice of court injunctions, however, and insisted on driving past her house and acting in a bullish, threatening way towards the poor girl. Another complaint was made, and Stuart ended up in court where he was given a six-week prison sentence.

It was a sobering moment for my brother. I hated the thought of him banged up, and although I could not argue that it wasn't the right thing, I wanted to do my best for him, to help him through this difficult time, even if it was of his own making. He would call me regularly from prison, telling me how much he hated it there, but that it had forced him to see he needed to make a drastic change in his life.

'I've worked hard, Jayne,' he would say. 'I've worked hard to make a better life than the one we grew up in, but I'm losing it all.' It broke my heart to hear him say it. I knew more than anyone that he could be loving and caring and kind, and I had watched helplessly as the brother I had loved so much had changed beyond recognition.

But prison had given him time to reflect, as on his release there seemed to be a new determination about my brother. He got back to work and focused on building a decent life for himself. Prison had changed him. Made him into a better person, or so I thought. It really looked to me as if my brother had turned a corner.

As I still lived in London and Stuart in Buckinghamshire, we spoke regularly – daily almost – on the phone. Happy or sad, he would call me up, and now and then I felt as if I was becoming his counsellor. Certainly I was his confidante, secret-keeper to his woes, his hopes and his fears; and I was happy to be so. There had been a time when such phone calls had been terribly difficult for me, as he confessed all his failings and acknowledged that he was turning into a monster, but after his spell in prison there was a new quality to his voice, a confidence and a happiness that reminded me of the little boy of my childhood.

I was still in bed one morning not long after my third child, Bethany, was born when Stuart called me up sounding happier than ever.

'I've met someone, Jayne,' he told me, almost breathlessly.

I smiled when I heard his voice. It was so excited, the voice of a teenager again. 'Really?' I asked. 'What's her name?'

'Vicky.'

I paused for a moment. 'Another Vicky?' I asked lightly.

'Yeah,' Stuart told me, not commenting on the irony. 'She's right posh!' he told me, and I laughed. 'Wait till you hear her voice, Jayne. Just wait till you hear it. I actually want to sleep with her voice!'

'Stuart!' I exclaimed, but there was no stopping him.

'You've got to meet her, Jayne. She's spectacular. She *speaks* beautiful, and she *is* beautiful . . .'

It was a joy for me to hear him like this, but as before

with Stuart there was a nagging worry in the back of my mind about how everything was going to pan out.

'I'm happy for you, Stu,' I told him. 'I really am. Just make sure you don't mess it up, OK? Knuckle down, do your job, don't get into fights . . .'

'No, no, Jayne,' he interrupted me, 'course not. But listen, you've got to meet her. I'm bringing her round to see you.'

'All right, Stuart,' I said with a laugh, 'but give me plenty of warning, won't you, so I can make sure the house is clean.'

'Oh, shut up, Jayne,' he laughed. 'Your house is always clean.' And he hung up on me.

I got out of bed and started getting the children ready for the day, but about an hour after I had finished my conversation with Stuart, there was a knock on the door. My brow furrowed as I wondered who could possibly be calling round at this time in the morning. Blearily I opened it, and there he was, a big, childish grin on his face. Next to him was one of the loveliest women I had ever seen. I looked at her in shock, my hands involuntarily moving to my straggly, uncombed hair and un-made-up face. I blushed when I realised I was standing there in mismatched pyjamas while the woman in front of me looked glamorous and perfect.

'Jayne,' Stuart said, 'meet Vicky.'

'Oh,' I said, totally deflated because of my appearance. 'Hi. Come in.' And together they crossed the threshold into my house.

It is one of those memories that I relive over and over, like a pleasant dream that turns into a recurring nightmare. How I wish I could go back to that moment and tell my former self not to let her in. To send her from my door and tell her that she should never approach me or my brother again. To tell her that we did not want her in our lives any more than she wanted us in hers. That this was a mistake. The worst mistake she could ever make.

But I can't go back in time. I can't change the past. Just as I am forced to relieve my childhood like a helpless observer gazing through a windowpane, so I am forced to relive the moment that that beautiful, kind, sparkling, fun woman walked into my life, and the unspeakable, tragic, horrible events followed . . .

# 10
## *Vicky*

Vicky Walton was every bit as wonderful as my brother had described her. If anything, he hadn't done her justice.

Slim and beautiful, she had lustrous blonde hair cut into a short bob, and piercing blue eyes that sparkled every time her massive smile spread across her face. And on the first day I met her, that infectious smile was always there. Stuart was smiling too, and it lit up his whole face as they sat together in my sitting room, hand in hand. It was immediately clear to me, as it would have been to anyone who saw them together, that they were entirely besotted with each other.

Her voice was clear and, unlike mine and Stuart's, well-to-do. Her clothes were immaculate, not that it would have mattered – she was the sort of person who could have worn an old black bin-liner and still looked fabulous. When she chatted, it was like the sun coming out: she was so funny and witty that she brightened up the room whenever she spoke. She had class and style. I fell for her as instantly as Stuart had, and while he sat there looking like the cat that had got the cream, I felt a thrill as I wondered whether he had finally found his soul mate; I forced myself not to listen to the nagging doubt in the back of my head that he would somehow, sometime, mess it all up for himself and those around him.

Vicky and I became close from that first meeting. We were kindred spirits, two people who found a common bond. I was entranced by her quietly spoken nature, which belied an intelligence and a forthrightness that few people display. Dear though my brother was to me, I was not blind to his faults, and I often found myself wondering just what it was in him she saw: there was something about her that made you think she would be better suited to someone other than a working-class bricklayer with a history of violence. But there was no question that she loved my brother. Perhaps the very fact that he was rough around the edges was what attracted her to him. Perhaps she, like me, saw the other side to his nature, the vulnerability that existed beneath the abrasive shell. They looked like an odd couple, the gentle Vicky and the boisterous Stuart, but they were infatuated with each other.

From the time we met, I chatted with Vicky even more than with Stuart. One day, early on in their relationship, we were gossiping away, and she gazed straight into my eyes with that piercing, insightful look of hers.

'Stuart's told me a lot about you, Jayne,' she said. 'He

told me that you've come a long way, that you've changed a lot since you were a little girl.'

'I *have* changed,' I said, momentarily taken aback by Vicky's perception. 'But I suppose you do change when you have kids, don't you?'

She smiled warmly at me. 'I suppose so,' she said quietly.

I wondered if I should tell her more, tell her about the changes I had gone through since I was a child, of all the horrific things that had happened. Out of all the people I had met before, somehow I thought I would feel most comfortable telling her. But close as I felt to her, I decided against it. Stuart didn't know of Graham's abuse, and Vicky would surely tell him if I confessed it to her, so I kept quiet. Instead, I decided to probe her a little, to satisfy my curiosity about her feelings for my brother, and if necessary to warn her of what he could be like. I didn't want to ruin anything for them, but I thought it only right that she should know the truth about him.

'So,' I asked, 'what about you and Stuart, then?'

It was a vague question, but Vicky saw through it straight away, immediately understanding what I was really asking her and seemingly unconcerned that I might be interfering in any way.

'I absolutely love your brother, Jayne,' she told me simply in a plain tone of voice that left me in no doubt that she was telling the truth. 'He's so funny and so lovely.'

'But you do know, don't you –' I chose my words carefully – 'that he's been in trouble with the police?'

Vicky shrugged it off lightly. 'Oh, yes,' she said. 'I know about that. He told me early on, but I don't care. I'm not that narrow-minded. He loves me, Jayne, and I love him. Very much.'

And to see the two of them together, it was impossible to doubt.

We would chat on the phone most days, and Vicky would tell me about her past. Her parents had split up when she was very young, and she missed her father dreadfully, though she was close to her mother and her younger sister, Emma. I would tell her in roundabout ways of the insecurities I experienced growing up – all the while avoiding admitting the truth about Graham – and she listened with the practised ear of a true friend.

As Vicky and Stuart got closer, so she became more of a sister to me, and our conversations would become more personal and more troubled. Vicky confided in me that, although she loved Stuart more than anything, her family did not approve of the relationship. She came from a comfortable middle-class family. But Stuart was just a bricklayer, a labourer with a sometimes troubled recent past.

'It's not me, Jayne,' she would assure me. 'I love him to bits and he treats me like royalty. We couldn't be happier. I just wish other people could see him for what he really is.'

In a way I could understand that there were people who would be less than thrilled that someone like Vicky would be going out with someone like Stuart. But I regretted it too, because I knew how sensitive he was. He already had a problem with his own self-esteem, and the idea that other people might not like him only added to that. Vicky was sensitive too: she wanted everyone to be as happy for her as she was, and could not understand it when they failed to be so. The two of them would often come and stay with me for the weekend, and to some it might have seemed odd that they would come to crowded, urban East London in an attempt to get away from the more rural environment of Buckinghamshire; but I think they just wanted to be with people who didn't judge them, and who took them for what they were.

It was no surprise to me, a few months into their relationship, that they announced their engagement. They had already moved in together, and were so well suited to each other, so in love, that it seemed only natural that they would want to start making long-term plans for a future together. As soon as it was decided that they were to get married, Vicky was on the phone to me, gossiping and excited. She didn't want anything extravagant, she told me: a simple white dress, a buffet at the local pub and a few bottles of champagne. No fuss; nothing showy. It was to be about the commitment she and Stuart were making, and about having those closest to them all around in order to share their good fortune. I had never seen them happier than they were on their wedding day: they were giggling like schoolchildren, so in thrall to each other that they seemed almost oblivious to the people who had come to celebrate with them. I couldn't help myself smiling every time I looked at them; and the smile came back to my face every time I thought about them in the days that followed.

After the wedding, they revelled in domesticity. Not all the time – they were a fun-loving couple who liked to go out a lot – but more than once I would have one or the other of them calling me up asking for advice about cooking, which was not something either of them had a particular talent for. They would each ask me for recipes so that they could treat and impress the other, sometimes not even realising that the other had done exactly the same thing earlier that day. On one occasion, Stuart called me to say that he had picked a bowlful of plums from a tree in the garden. 'I've got these plums, Jayne,' he told me not at all sheepishly, 'and I want to make a nice plum crumble and custard. How do I go about it?'

I told him what to do, and off he went to make Vicky plum crumble for her Sunday lunch. I swear that for months later I was hearing about what a fantastic plum crumble that was, and in my quieter moments I would reflect on how he had been boasting about his culinary achievements with the same verve that he used to boast about his fighting. If ever there was proof that Vicky was good for my brother, surely that was it.

He was good to her too. More than once my telephone would ring mid-morning on a Sunday and it would be Vicky. 'Guess where I am, Jayne,' she would say in a conspiratorial whisper.

'Where?' I would ask.

'In bed,' she told me. 'Still! And Stuart's downstairs cooking my lunch, and then we're going to the pub!' She sounded so thrilled that Stuart was treating her so well; and her pleasure was matched only by mine.

It sounds disloyal to say it, but even with the change in Stuart I never doubted that Vicky was too good for my brother. Despite that, however, she was a girl out for a good time, and that meant there were sides to her character that made me worried for her, not least the fact that she seemed to turn a blind eye to Stuart's fondness for cocaine.

My teenage experiments with drugs had gone out of the window the moment I first fell pregnant: there was no place for them in my life now that I had children around me. The fact that Vicky allowed Stuart to do coke was just about the only bone of contention that existed between the two of us, and I felt terrified every time I imagined the scene of him snorting the drug, as I knew he often did. But nobody lives a blameless life, and I could see that the positives of their relationship far outweighed that one negative. Stuart was sensitive enough to know never to do it in front of me – it was one of the unbreakable ground rules whenever he came to visit, and in any case he knew how nervous I was by that time whenever drugs were around.

The party lifestyle was never going to do Stuart any favours, though. The excessive drinking that he had previously become addicted to had subsided to an extent, but he still enjoyed a drink and it could not be controlled. During the honeymoon period of their relationship, his alcohol intake didn't really seem to be a problem – it was just part of the way of life they had together – but as time went on there began to be certain strains on the marriage, strains that Stuart was ill-equipped to cope with. Before she moved in with Stuart, Vicky had lived at home with her mum and sister. As they did not really approve of Stuart, Vicky, I think, felt guilty about leaving them to live with him. It put a pressure on their relationship. When they were with me it was all I could do to stop them putting their hands all over each other, whereas when they were with Vicky's family, they felt the need to play down their mutual love and affection, which had an effect on Stuart's insecurities.

Gradually but inevitably Stuart fell back into his old ways of drinking. The worse it got, the more I started to worry about what my brother was capable of; but it was something of a mixed blessing when Vicky finally put her foot down about it. She threatened to leave him unless he cut his alcohol intake, and the threat was enough to rein Stuart in for a little while. To my horror, however, she told him that even though he had stopped drinking he could continue to do cocaine. I was furious, and I told her so: all he was doing was swapping one habit for another, but Stuart liked it too much and there was no way he was going to stop.

Alcohol, drugs, insecurities: these were things that were always going to send Stuart back to his old ways, and I lived with an ever-present dread that tempered the happiness I felt because he and Vicky were together. One day, I knew, it would go wrong.

That day came soon enough.

Jealousy is a terrible thing, and it was an emotion Stuart struggled with. If ever Vicky was getting ready to go out for the night by herself, she would have to put up with Stuart hanging around asking her unpleasant questions. 'What are you dressing up like that for?' he would ask. 'You going out to find yourself a new boyfriend or something?' And she would have to do her very best to persuade him that she only had eyes for him, that he was the only one in her life.

But the green-eyed monster had shown itself, and it would not go away.

It was only a few months after their wedding that my phone rang late one evening. It was Vicky in floods of tears, almost unable to speak between sobs.

'What's the matter, Vicky?' I urged, terrible scenarios playing themselves out in my head. 'What's happened?'

'You're not going to believe it,' she wailed. 'It's Stuart. He hit me. He punched me in the face.'

I felt as if I myself had been struck a blow in the stomach. Whenever I heard about domestic violence, it brought all the old fears back. I would be in the room again with Graham, waiting for him to rape me; or cowering before my abusive boyfriend. The fact that it was Vicky, my surrogate sister, suffering at the hands of my brother made it a hundred times worse.

'Oh, Vicky,' I whispered. 'What happened?'

Gaining control of her tears, she explained. The two of them had gone out for a pizza, an innocent enough night out and one that neither of them thought would mark a change in their relationship. As they were chatting, they started talking about a boyfriend of Vicky's, who had been on the scene around the time that she met my brother. Stuart had started asking questions about him, saying to Vicky that she shouldn't worry about telling the truth, that they shouldn't have any secrets from each other. Poor Vicky, ever honest, took him at his word and confessed that she had kissed this man after she had started going with Stuart.

She soon realised her mistake.

Stuart went mad, consumed by anger and jealousy. He flipped, and when they got home he hit her across the side of the face with one of the crushing blows so many unfortunate people had been on the receiving end of any number of times previously. It must have seemed to Vicky that her whole world had been swept from under her feet.

'Listen to me, Vicky,' I told her. 'I know he's my brother, but he can't get away with this. Go to the hospital, tell them who did it. And if you want to go to the police, I'll be a hundred per cent behind you.'

'No!' she replied sharply. 'No, I don't want to do that. It's my fault. I shouldn't have said anything.'

'It's *not* your fault, Vicky,' I assured her. 'I don't care what you said or what you did – nothing warrants that.'

I of all people, however, knew how difficult it is to stand up to that kind of treatment, or to admit to people in authority that you are at the receiving end of it. I knew she had to deal with it in her own way.

That didn't stop me from calling Stuart immediately, though. 'How dare you do that to her, Stuart? How *dare* you do what you've done?'

He had no satisfactory response. His voice was still

shaking with anger, and it was alarming to hear that he had not yet calmed down, that the fury that had arisen in him so suddenly had not abated with the same speed. I went to bed that night with a terrible foreboding.

The following week they came to London to see me. Stuart was full of remorse for his actions, promising me that he would never again lay a finger on Vicky; Vicky herself was prepared to forgive him. It worried me when she said that, because I knew that the more she forgave Stuart, the more he would believe he could get away with things. But I did my best to draw some comfort from the fact that they both genuinely wanted to make things right for each other that day. Perhaps, just perhaps, that would be an end to it.

But it wasn't an end. It was just the beginning.

From that moment on, something changed in their relationship. It wasn't that they were any less in love with each other, or any less attracted to each other. Theirs was a complicated bond, however: when it was loving, it was the best imaginable, but when it was fiery, it was over the top. If they had an argument, it would be explosive and aggressive – they would be scary to be around. And of course, now that the seal had been broken on Stuart's violent nature, it continued. After practically every argument they ever had, Vicky would be on the phone to me in floods of tears, telling me what had happened. More often than not, they would have got into a flaming row about Stuart wanting to go down to the pub without her, and Vicky would quite rightly be worried about how his drinking binge would end. Vicky told me that Stuart would start poking her viciously, goading her with his words and his actions, occasionally driving her to such a level of frustration that she would end up slapping him across the face. It saddened me when she told me of this, because I was sure that before she met Stuart, Vicky had never laid a finger on anyone in her whole life, and I hated the thought of my brother's cycle of violence extending to his wife.

Stuart's retaliations, of course, would be brutal. He would storm through the house, smashing things against the wall before turning his attention to Vicky. He would lay into her, saying the most horrible things, tormenting her about her family. Sometimes it would just be petty – if she wanted to sleep, he would play music loudly to keep her awake; he would poke her roughly and tug at her hair just to annoy and upset her. They lived on a knife edge of violence.

I would take Stuart to task for what he did. My loathing of conflict was more acute now than it had ever been, and this was conflict between two people I loved so much. 'If it carries on, Stuart,' I told him on more than one occasion, 'if you ever hit her again, I'll tell Vicky to leave you, and I'll see to it that she gets all the help she needs.'

That one threat was enough to reduce him to tears. He could see what was happening just as well as I could. One day he sat before me, his head in his hands, shaking uncontrollably.

'What am I going to do, Jayne?' he asked me. 'What am I going to do to stop myself becoming what I'm becoming? I know it's wrong. I saw it all happening when we were growing up and I detest it. I don't want to be this person . . .'

I stared at him with a curious mixture of pity, love and horror, remembering the little boy from my childhood who used to look after me so fiercely.

*Suddenly I am back at home in Larne.*

*I look at my brother. He is only young, but his face is filled with a fury that he does not understand as the bullies taunt him and he is forced to stick up for himself.*

*And now I see him as an adult – an adult who still does not fully understand the things that go through his mind, the emotions that take control of him. The little boy who looked after me has turned into a violent man. I hate it; but perhaps I am also beginning to understand it.*

I looked at my brother, trying not to let the loathing I felt for his violence show in my face.

'Go and get counselling,' I told him flatly. 'Get help.'

But he poured scorn on my suggestion. 'I'm not getting counselling,' he scowled. 'Counselling's for idiots.'

'I had counselling,' I reminded him.

'That's different. You're a woman. Counselling's not for men. It's not for me.' And nothing I could say would persuade him otherwise. He was totally honest with me, and admitted that he could not go into counselling because if anyone found out they would think he was weak, and that was the one thing he couldn't bear.

And so the cycle of violence continued, as it always will if something is not done to stop it. How well I knew its workings; and yet I felt helpless to do anything. Besides that, I was occupied with my growing family, especially after the birth of my fourth child, Alyce.

As time passed, Vicky and Stuart started having little trial separations. These separations were difficult for both of them. Vicky would be on the phone to me telling me how fed up she was without him, and then Stuart would call me. 'I really love her, Jayne,' he would tell me plainly, with a haunted tone to his voice.

'I know, Stu,' I'd tell him. 'But you're treating her wrong.'

'What can I do to get her back?'

I sighed. 'You can't keep buying her flowers, Stu. You've got to show her in your actions that you really mean it.'

He finally agreed to go with Vicky to see a marriage guidance counsellor; but their sessions with the counsellor were characteristically tempestuous. When they were over, I would get phone calls from the both of them, each claiming that the counsellor had taken their side and believed them to be in the right, but neither of them seeming to have derived any real benefit from it. But then, an hour later, I would get a phone call from one or other of them telling me how in love they were. It was intense and wild and unpredictable, and I feel sure that the rollercoaster of their emotions was as inexplicable to them as it was to me.

If ever there was a time that none of us wanted Graham and the poison he could distribute back in our lives, this was it.

Although his face and actions continued to haunt my darkest moments, Graham himself had not played a huge part in any of our lives since I left home. But he kept in occasional contact with other members of the family, who had no reason to ban him from their lives because they did not know what he had done to me. And although Stuart and he were never the best of friends, they did have intermittent contact.

I never did get to the bottom of what Graham said or did to Stuart that started off what happened next. I assumed it was something to do with money. Maybe Graham had wound him up at the wrong time – never something you wanted to do with Stuart. Whatever it was, all I know is that one day Stuart was fuming about something that involved my abuser. Graham had made Vicky angry too.

'I don't like that guy,' she told my brother. 'He's a total prat and I've never trusted him.'

Stuart was on the warpath. Given the chance, he would have done to Graham what he did the night so many years ago when he discovered my babysitter beating me with a wet towel; and I, for one, despite my loathing of violence, would not have lost much sleep over my abuser receiving some kind of retribution. What I couldn't bear, however, was the idea of Stuart being plunged into another violent scenario; and I didn't want him getting in trouble because of Graham. That man had brought enough misery on our family; I didn't want any more.

I did my best to persuade Stuart to leave it alone, but I was fighting a losing battle. Vicky told me that my brother and Graham would argue on the phone, and Graham would goad Stuart, winding him up. It was almost as though he knew that the more he taunted him, the more likely it was that Stuart would get himself in trouble.

I couldn't stand by and let that happen.

It was in a moment of madness that I decided to call him up. Quite calmly I asked Vicky to give me Graham's number.

'What for, Jayne?' she asked.

'Just give it to me, Vicky,' I replied in a flat tone of voice, and she did.

It was almost in a dreamlike state that I dialled his number.

I felt in control. Powerful, almost.

Under any other circumstances I would have done whatever was in my power to avoid having any kind of contact with him, but this involved Stuart and Vicky, the two people – aside from my husband, Simon and my children – whom I loved more than anyone in the world. I had realised, in a moment of sudden clarity, that I had a hold over him. Or so I thought.

'Yeah?' His voice was curt when he answered the phone, and I suppressed a shiver of loathing.

'Hello, Graham,' I said quietly. 'It's me. Jayne.'

For a moment he didn't answer. And then, quietly, 'What do you want?'

'I'll tell you what I want, Graham. I want you to leave Stuart alone. Stay away from him and Vicky. Stop winding them up.'

He started to speak, but I interrupted him.

'And if you don't, I swear to God I'm going to go to the police and tell them that you raped me.'

A silence. And then he spoke.

'You're sick,' he said. 'I can't believe you would say such a sordid, disgusting thing. You're really warped.'

I was staggered by his response. Speechless. Breathless. I simply didn't know what to say, so I slammed the phone down. My body was shaking now, and I had the horrible feeling that I had just made a dreadful mistake.

What the hell had I been thinking of?

I sat in silence for five minutes before the phone rang again. Tentatively, I answered.

It was Vicky. Her voice sounded perplexed. 'I've just had a really strange phone call, Jayne,' she told me.

'What?' I asked. 'Who?'

'Graham told me that you accused him of being a rapist.'

I closed my eyes and took a deep breath. 'You'd better put Stuart on the phone,' I said quietly, and I prepared myself for the scene that was to follow.

Stuart's voice was shaky when he came on the line. 'What's going on, Jayne?' he asked.

'Listen carefully, Stuart,' I told him. 'I don't want you to be angry, I don't want you to go fighting, and I want you to work on building your relationship with Vicky. Do you understand?'

He spoke as though he hadn't heard a word I said. 'What have you got to tell me, Jayne?'

I steeled myself. 'Stuart, when we were kids, something happened. When we were growing up, Graham used to rape me, regularly. It went on for several years.'

We both fell silent.

I could hear Stuart's breath on the other end of the phone. It was heavy and shaky. And then he shouted.

'That's it, Jayne! I'm going round there, now! I'm going to fucking kill the bastard. Kill him!' There were tears of rage in his voice, and I recognised the sound of him losing control.

'Stuart!' I said firmly. 'Listen to me. I'm sorry you had to find out like this. But you've got to understand that this happened a long time ago. It's something I've come to terms with.'

'But I can't believe it!' he yelled. 'I can't believe he's done this.'

'He has,' I said, 'but it's over. You've got to realise, though, that he destroys everything he touches. He's doing it to you now. If you want to deal with him, go to the police, but don't do anything stupid and let him ruin your life like he ruined mine.'

He was raving now, tearful and angry, and I wasn't getting through to him. There was nothing I could say to console him, and I was absolutely shattered, angry with myself that I had revealed the truth in such a way, and in so doing shaken the world of the brother I loved so much. It was the worst thing I could have done. I saw that now.

'You'd better speak to Vicky,' he told me.

She came on the line. The shock and pity in her voice was heartbreaking to hear. 'I can't believe it,' she cried. 'I just want to be there with you now to give you a big hug.'

'Listen to me, Vicky,' I said. 'I don't want anybody doing anything on my behalf. Promise me, Vicky, that you and Stu won't do anything?' I begged.

'I'll do my best, Jayne,' Vicky told me, but I knew she would have a fight on her hands; I could hear Stuart in the background, crashing around. I felt absolutely terrible. I had devastated Stuart and Vicky with my mistimed confession, and that was the last thing in the world that I had wanted to do. All I had tried to do was help, but it had gone so horribly wrong. What had I been thinking of? How would it end?

That night I experienced once more all the feelings of self-loathing and disgust that I had endured as a child. Talking about it had brought it all back. But on top of that, I was full of concern for Stuart and Vicky and what they must be feeling, how they would be dealing with this new information – so familiar to me yet so shocking to them.

I might have guessed that Stuart would hit the bottle.

He got blind drunk. Throughout the evening he kept phoning me, each time more boozed-up and tearful than the last.

'You were everything to me, Jayne,' he slurred. 'You *are* everything. I can't believe he did that and I didn't know. We tell each other everything. Why didn't you tell me?' He sounded so let down by me and that, I think, was the worst thing of all.

'I'm sorry,' was all I could think of saying. How could I explain the complicated, warped emotions I had experienced as a child; how Graham had made me feel it was all my fault, that I was a dirty, worthless girl?

And then it came, as I feared it would. 'I'm going to go up there,' he said, 'to his house, and I'm going to rip that cunt's heart out of his chest, and I'm going to shove it in his mouth.'

The sound of his voice – full of fury – was terrifying. I truly believed that he was going to do exactly that.

'I'm in the car now!' he shouted. 'I'm going to do it.'

'Stuart,' I cried, 'I'm begging you. If you love me, you won't do this. *Please.*'

But he was growing madder and madder. 'You can't ask that of me!' he yelled. 'You think you can control me, but you can't!'

I was frantic now. 'Stuart,' I begged, 'this guy destroyed my life. Don't let him destroy yours. *Don't do this.*'

Suddenly, down the phone, there was a roar of frustration. 'Aaaarrrgghhh!!!' he shouted. Then there was a screeching of the car brakes, followed by a horrible crunch. I found out later that he had driven his car straight into a tree.

An awful, ominous silence followed.

'Stuart!' I shouted. 'What's happened? Stuart, are you there?'

When he finally spoke, his voice was woozy. 'I can't

believe you're making me do this, Jayne. I can't believe you're making me leave him alone. I want to hate you, but I can't because I love you too much.'

I was overcome by relief and exhaustion. He was OK, and he wasn't going to go through with his threat. Not tonight at least.

'I love you too, Stu,' I said. 'I love you too.'

For the following few days and weeks, all I could do was apologise. But the next time Stuart and Vicky came to see me, they arrived on my doorstep with a big bunch of flowers. As soon as he came in, Stuart enveloped me in a big hug.

'I'm going to do what you ask,' he told me. 'I'm not going to touch him, because he's not worth it. But listen –' he looked me straight in the eyes '– we don't keep any secrets from each other any more. OK?'

I smiled weakly at him. 'OK, Stuart,' I said. 'No more secrets. I promise. I'm sorry.'

# 11

## *The Breakdown*

There is no doubt in my mind that Stuart's discovery of what Graham had done to me was the catalyst for everything that happened next.

The fact that he had been unable to do anything to stop what had happened, and that I had forbidden him to inflict his own retribution upon my abuser, ate away at him. More than once he cried in front of me; more than once I heard him hitting his head against the phone in anger and frustration.

'It's too horrible, Jayne,' he would weep. 'I can't get it out of my head. I can't believe I haven't punished him and it's become an obsession. It's affecting my marriage. It's affecting *everything*.'

I did my best to console him, but I could see that it was useless. I had lived with this knowledge for many years; for Stuart it was new, fresh and raw. And, to my horror and heartbreak, I saw that it was indeed having an effect on his marriage.

Volatility was the defining feature of my brother's

relationship with his new wife. One minute they would be laughing about something, the next they would be at each other's throats about it. Gradually it became clear that they would use any stick to beat each other with, regardless of the seriousness of the problem. On one occasion, Stuart did some work for a man who said he could get hold of a gun if he wanted it. I knew nothing about guns – all I was told was that it was the sort for shooting pigeons and the like. I didn't approve – I thought it was a terrible idea for anyone to have a gun in the house, least of all Stuart. But when I spoke to Vicky about it she laughed it off, as if it was some big joke.

'That's sick, Vicky,' I told her in disgust. 'Why would anyone want a gun?'

But she didn't take my anxieties seriously, and that was that.

It was some time later that the issue of the gun came up again. Stuart and Vicky had an argument and the gun had become a bone of contention. The argument escalated as arguments will – especially when Stuart was involved – and he threatened to shoot her.

An alarm bell rang in my mind when Vicky recounted the conversation to me and she told me that her response had been: 'Oh just shoot me now, and put me out of my misery'. It wasn't that I took Stuart seriously; even though I hated the idea of him having a gun, I knew he was too besotted with Vicky ever to go through with a crazy, thoughtless threat like that. It was the fact that Vicky's response sounded to me more like something Stuart himself would say, almost as though a little bit of Stuart's dark side had rubbed off on her.

It was a horrible thought, but I put it from my mind, along with my worries about Stuart being in possession of the gun at all. I never heard either of them mention it again.

The arguments, however, continued. They grew worse and worse, increasing both in frequency and in severity. When Christmas 2002 came round, Stuart and Vicky became so furious with each other that they wrecked their own Christmas tree, decorations and all, during one of their fights. Of course, I ended up on the phone with them, doing my best to act as a mediator. I refused to hang up until they had reconstructed the tree and I could hear them talking to each other in a civil way. It set the tone for many phone calls to come: if either of them called me in the heat of an argument, I would never let the conversation end until the argument had diffused and they were communicating properly. What else could I do?

I couldn't be there for them all the time, though, and it was no surprise to me when Vicky finally went to the police. She and Stuart had been in bed, she told them, and in a rage Stuart had stubbed a lighted cigarette out on her leg. Stuart denied it, of course, saying it had just been a clumsy accident, but Vicky pressed charges and Stuart was found guilty of assault. He was sentenced to three months in prison, and was sent to HMP Bullingdon in Oxfordshire.

I felt distraught that it had come to this, but I was relieved at least that Vicky had had the strength to stand up to Stuart and his violent ways. It was not until Stuart was safely behind bars, however, that I discovered all was not as it seemed. Stuart had indeed burned Vicky's leg with a cigarette, but she knew full well that it had not been on purpose – just an accident as he was reaching out for something. Vicky was sheepish when she admitted this, but she told me she had been at her wits' end with all the arguments and the cruelty and violence. I believed her: I could hear the guilt in her voice, and sense that she was beating herself up over what she had done. In her own way she tried to make things right again, every single day sending Stuart little presents and loving notes to help him through his time inside, but I think she knew that she really had to tell him the truth – that she knew, on this occasion at least, he had not set out to hurt her.

'But he'll go mad, Jayne,' she fretted. 'I'm scared to tell him. I don't know what he'll do.'

I disagreed. 'You know what, Vicky?' I told her. 'The way his mind is at the moment, I think he'll just laugh it off.'

And that's what he did.

On the day he came out, Vicky sprinkled the bed with

rose petals and wrapped up a special gift for every week that he had been in prison. Then she sat him down and told him the truth. As I thought he might do, Stuart simply started laughing. 'I can't believe you did that!' he exclaimed as Vicky hung her head, embarrassed but pleased that he had not taken it too badly. Such was Stuart's unpredictability.

The arguments soon started up again, however – clearly Vicky's tactic had failed to have its desired effect – and now Stuart had another verbal stick to beat her with. 'You sent me to prison, you cow! That's the sort of bitch you are.' There wasn't much she could say to that, but knowing Vicky I've no doubt she gave as good as she got.

It was perhaps a sign of their up-and-down relationship, however, when Vicky, out of the blue, made a demand.

'I want to renew my wedding vows,' she told Stuart.

It was typical of their relationship, which went from depths of violence to the heights of infatuation, and Stuart agreed with her idea eagerly. Their actual marriage had been in a register office and a pub, and Vicky had been dreaming of renewing their vows with a proper white wedding with all the frills and the ceremony that went with it. I suppose she also knew that Stuart's first wedding had been a lavish occasion, and she wanted what his first wife had been given. There would be a horse and carriage, and there would be a marquee.

Somewhat to my surprise, Stuart threw himself into the

notion with enthusiasm. Despite everything, he loved Vicky and Vicky loved him. It would be perfect, and when Vicky called to ask me if I would be her maid of honour along with her sister, Emma, I agreed with pride. Stuart asked my son, Luke, if he would be his page boy and dress up with him in top hat and tails, and the suit fittings were soon arranged. Vicky threw herself into the arrangements, searching for venues, planning, dreaming. Every idea she had for the wedding was perfect, and she appeared to me to be more radiant than she had been for years. Since the time she had met Stuart, she had kept a small clipping of her dream wedding dress in a drawer; now she got it out again and started making arrangements for a dressmaker to put it together for her.

All this, of course, came at a price. Almost daily I would get a call from Vicky, gobsmacked by the cost of the marquee or the horse and carriage, but excited nevertheless and determined that mere finances would not get in the way of her perfect day.

Stuart was a bit more worried about how all this was to be paid for. In addition, Vicky had planned the event for the August of 2004; Stuart, though, had got the wrong end of the stick and had understood it was to be the June of the following year. When he discovered his mistake, he suddenly put the brakes on.

'Hang on,' he told Vicky, 'not only am I supposed to be

spending all this money on renewing our wedding vows, but we've only got until this August to raise the money. And if you want the perfect wedding, we've got to have the perfect honeymoon too.'

All of a sudden, what should have been a happy flurry of preparations started turning into a nightmare. Stuart would call me in floods of tears saying, 'I want to renew my vows with her, Jayne. I love her – but this is putting too much pressure on me.'

Then Vicky would start bending my ear: 'I want to do this now,' she told me adamantly. 'I'm not doing it if I have to wait – it wouldn't mean anything then.'

Things grew more intense; tempers became more fraught; the relationship between Stuart and Vicky's family deteriorated. My brother started to get paranoid that their influence over Vicky was greater than his own. It became an obsession with him. The strain on Vicky was enormous: she would dissolve in floods of tears at the drop of a hat, and she and Stuart decided any number of times to split up and then they'd get back together again. As was so often the case with those two, what should have been a happy time became destructive and upsetting.

In reality, of course, Stuart was getting nervous. He didn't like being rushed; he didn't like not being in control. The result was predictable: his drinking increased. He couldn't cope with the stress, he couldn't cope with the wedding-vow talk, he couldn't cope with the family disagreements. Truth be told, by this stage he couldn't cope with life. And whereas Vicky was prepared to have her dream wedding at any cost, he tried to distance himself from it by losing his troubles in an ocean of alcohol, as an ostrich sticks its head in the sand. One night he got home so blind drunk that an argument was inevitable. This one was worse than most, however, and culminated in a drunken Stuart driving his car into Vicky's.

A few days later, they argued again about the wedding-vow preparations. Distraught by Stuart's attitude, Vicky stormed out, leaving my brother to stew in his own juice. No doubt he started drinking again because while she was out of the house, Stuart had an argument with a neighbour.

Even in the state he was in, somewhere deep down I think Stuart knew that getting violent with an old lady wasn't on. As soon as the argument with the neighbour was over, he called me.

'You'd better call Vicky now, Jayne.'

'Why?' I asked him. 'What have you done?'

'Had an argument with our neighbour.'

My heart sank. 'What did you say to her, Stu?'

'Well,' he replied, 'it's a bit awkward. I told her to shut her fucking mouth and threw a can of beer at her.'

I agreed to call Vicky for him, but not before telling him

what I thought of the situation. 'You've got to learn to control your temper, Stuart,' I said.

'Yeah, but she's been getting on my nerves for ages. I've had enough.' He didn't sound like he had even registered what I said.

I called Vicky as I'd promised I would. She was having lunch somewhere.

'Look, Vicky,' I told her. 'I know you and Stuart are having a few difficulties at the moment, but you've got a bit of a problem at home.' I explained what had happened.

Vicky was furious, and I didn't blame her. 'That's it, Jayne,' she told me. 'I've had enough. I've had it with him.' She sounded like she meant it.

I don't know what would have happened had the police not intervened. Perhaps Vicky would have kicked Stuart out of the house, but in the event the neighbour quite reasonably took out an injunction against him that meant he could not come within a certain distance of her. As a result, Stuart found himself legally obliged to move out of the marital home. He found a room to rent in a house a couple of streets away from where they lived.

In a way, this was what the two of them had been waiting for: the perfect opportunity for a trial separation. Anyone who knew them could see how volatile and potentially explosive their relationship was; anyone could see that they loved each other and wound each other up in equal measure. Time apart was what they needed – not a day or two here and there as they had occasionally done in the past – but the real thing. Time apart to reflect and to make them realise – to make *Stuart* realise – what they had together, and what he was compromising with his arguments and his violence.

The day he moved into his room, my brother called me up. He sounded quite upbeat. 'Don't worry, Jayne,' he told me, 'I've got the best of both worlds now. I can drink whenever I want without getting grief, and Vicky can come round here so I can have a shag whenever I want to!'

'As long as you're OK,' I told him, a bit primly perhaps, and wondering if my brother might just have missed the point. But when I spoke to Vicky later the same day, she said pretty much the same thing.

'It's great, Jayne. I can do what I want, but I get to sleep with him whenever I fancy it.'

'A bit too much information, Vicky,' I told her with a smile.

Not long after Stuart moved out of the marital home, his mother-in-law moved in to help Vicky. What started as a strangely convenient arrangement soon became less so. Vicky told me that she would tell her mum she was going out with friends, but really she was nipping round to see Stuart. Despite this secrecy, she sounded as though the enforced separation was doing them good. 'I do still love your brother,' she told me, 'and we are still planning the wedding.' And when I spoke to Stuart, he simply reiterated what Vicky had said. I remember being slightly worried that their entire relationship at that time had been reduced to a sexual one, with precious little else to bolster it or back it up; but they were being nice to each other; they were communicating. It seemed like progress.

I should have known that the progress would last only a few days.

For Stuart, I think the novelty of being on his own soon wore off, and he started wanting to see his wife more often than she wanted to see him. Even though Vicky would occasionally sneak round to see him without her mum knowing, it wasn't enough.

He would phone me up at three in the morning, blind drunk and tearful. 'I want to see my wife, Jayne. I can't stand the fact that her mum's seeing Vicky more than I am. It's just not fair. She's keeping Vicky away from me.'

'Don't be stupid, Stuart,' I told him. 'Of course she's not.' But he refused to listen to reason – he was too far gone for that. I didn't dare say to him that even if Vicky's mum had taken against him, I wouldn't blame her for it after the way he had been treating her daughter.

For a week I spent my time trying to persuade Stuart not to get so obsessive about things but it was difficult. When

Vicky was at home she started avoiding Stuart's calls. If she did speak to him on the phone, Stuart complained that she was a different person. Maybe it was an attempt to prove her independence to those around her, but it messed with Stuart's head. And Stuart's head, as we were soon tragically to find out, was not a thing to mess with.

A few days later, even the secret liaisons started to trail off, and Stuart's state of mind went from bad to worse. 'I hate her,' he told me down the phone, his voice full of bile. 'I'm going to go round there. I'm going to terrorise them. If they're going to make my life hell, I'm going to make it even worse for them.' His voice slurred as he spoke.

I begged him not to do anything stupid. 'I love you, Stuart. But I love Vicky too. If you do anything to hurt her, you'll be hurting me too, just the same as if you put your hand to me yourself. Please – don't do this.'

My words seemed to restrain him, but only just. 'You've got to speak to her,' he begged me. 'Stop her doing this to me.' I told him I would try, but in truth I didn't know what I could say to her. Poor Vicky was in an impossible position.

I asked Vicky if there was any way round the impasse in which they found themselves. 'I totally understand your situation,' I told her, 'but to be honest, I'm worried for you – I'm worried what Stuart will do if he's not allowed to see you. I'm worried he's going to start bullying you again.'

'He's not going to stand a chance this time,' Vicky

said with fire in her voice. 'If he starts, I'm calling the police.'

Half of me was glad to hear her talking like that; half of me was terrified to think what Stuart would do if he was provoked. I told her that if she wanted me to act as middle-man, to help them communicate, she only had to ask.

Stuart had been living on his own for about two weeks when Vicky finally agreed to go out with him for the day. She must have realised that it wasn't enough for them simply to have the occasional few hours of stolen time, for them to meet only to fulfil the physical side of their relationship at the expense of everything else – especially if they were going to go ahead and renew their wedding vows. And so she agreed that the following weekend she would spend the day with him: no sneaking around, no secrecy, just a man and his wife having some quality time. When the time approached, however, something came up. Perhaps Vicky had cold feet; perhaps she genuinely had an engagement she couldn't get out of. Whatever the truth of the matter, she cancelled.

Stuart was furious. I did my best to calm him down – I even told him that it was me who had suggested she cancel their date because I was sure Stuart would understand that. This wasn't true, of course, but I figured that if he thought that I was involved in some way, it would stop him from taking it out on Vicky. I knew Stuart would never hurt me, but he had taken his hand to Vicky more than once, and I couldn't bear to see that happen again.

Over the next few days I managed to get them to talk civilly to each other. Vicky apologised for cancelling and meekly said she was sorry if she had been nasty to Stuart; my brother seemed almost kittenish towards her. The cycle of their relationship had played itself out once more: the huge, explosive arguments and the hurt they inflicted on each other, followed by a period of peace when the love they each felt was obvious for anyone to see. I wondered at the time if the cycle would ever be broken.

'You know what it's like, Stuart,' Vicky told him. 'I just don't want the aggravation.'

'I know,' Stuart replied calmly, a different man from the drunken beast I had heard on the phone. 'I just miss you and I want to see you.'

It was on Wednesday, 2 June 2004 that Stuart called me in a state of high excitement. Vicky had agreed to spend some time with him that Sunday. How well I remember that phone call: the thrill in his voice, the way he almost seemed to tremble as he spoke. 'I'm going to see her, Jayne,' he enthused. 'We're going to spend the day together.' He told me of his plans, of how he was going to make it special for them both. He enthused; he sang her praises; he sounded like he was going to do the right thing.

Maybe, I thought, he had turned a corner.

Maybe he was going to make things work out between them.

Maybe everything was going to be all right.

## 12

# *Sunday, 6 June 2004*

Some days you just wake up feeling happy, as though nothing can dampen your mood or make your spirit heavy. Sunday, 6 June 2004 was one of those days.

I woke early, but rather than getting up straight away, I lay in bed for a while, enjoying the peace, thinking about the day ahead and looking forward to spending time with my family. I could already feel a warm breeze blowing through the open window in the bedroom I shared with my partner, Simon, and outside there was the sound of birds singing. I felt refreshed as I threw off the bed sheets and pulled back the curtains to look outside. The sky was blue and cloudless. It was going to be a beautiful day and I felt invigorated by that summery feeling.

My mobile rang at seven thirty in the morning. I saw it was Stuart but did not answer, deciding instead to wait until I had got my children up and ready for the day before embarking on a conversation with him. I didn't feel I was letting him down: I knew he would be happy and excited and was calling to share that with me. It wasn't like he needed my help. Not then.

I set the table for breakfast before going to wake the children, but before I had even finished putting bowls on the table, Luke, Bethany and Alyce had raced downstairs without me having to wake them. Their childish chatter filled the house. They too were excited that it was going to be such a lovely day – it meant that they would be able to play outside with their little friends from next door, and they were asking me even before they had eaten their cereals if they could have ice lollies. I smiled patiently at them, telling them it was too early for lollies, but we'd have to see about later on; and yes, they could go and see their friends but not yet as it was too early for that as well. They were full of life and boisterous – it was the sort of idyllic family moment that made everything else that had happened in my life seem unimportant. Seeing the joy on my children's faces made me feel a million miles from the traumas of my early life or the difficulties Stuart and Vicky were facing. There was no abuse here, or arguments, or violence. It was like one of those perfect moments I had acted out with my dollies all those years ago to protect me from the realities of my own childhood. All was as it should be.

When the children were dressed and had eaten breakfast, I saw to it that they had things to occupy them before telling them that I was going to call their Uncle Stuart. I predicted I might be on the phone with him for quite some time, and

I was right. He sounded ecstatically happy, and it was all I could do to stop him from talking and leave me to get on with what I had to do that day. It was the happiest I had heard him in a long time; perhaps it was naïve of me, but during that conversation any fears I had about his wellbeing seemed to vanish. 'You have a lovely day, Stu,' I said.

'Leave it to me, darling,' he told me. 'I'll phone you later and let you know how it went.'

I hung up, with a smile on my face.

The morning passed in a lazy way, as Sunday mornings will. The children played outside while I pottered around the house, preparing lunch but otherwise doing nothing in particular. My phone rang a few times during the morning, but no number was displayed and I ignored it, choosing instead to enjoy that precious time with my family. My eldest daughter, Emma, went out with friends, so Simon and I enjoyed having the little ones – Luke, Bethany and Alyce – around us.

At about one o'clock, I was chatting over the fence to our next-door neighbour about nothing in particular when my phone rang again. I smiled when I saw Stuart's number flash up on the screen. No doubt he was calling me, full of beans, to tell me what a fabulous day he was having. I put the phone to my ear and answered brightly, 'All right, Stu?'

In that moment, I knew my day was about to change.

I was so shocked when I heard Stuart's voice. I had expected to hear a happy man, as I had earlier that morning – light, thrilled and carefree. I couldn't have been more wrong. The person at the other end of the phone barely sounded like my brother. He sounded like a maniac. Angry. Crazed.

'Jayne!' he shouted. 'Is that you? Jayne!'

'Calm down, Stuart,' I said. 'Course it's me. What's the matter?'

'I hate her!' he yelled. 'I fucking *hate* her!'

An uncomfortable emotion rose in my chest – nervousness, I suppose. Apprehension. I knew my brother so well. I could read him like a book, and understood exactly what the different nuances in his voice indicated. There was something in the way he had spoken that was not unlike how he'd sounded the night I had told him about Graham's abuse. A desperate lack of control. His anger was rising, that terrible, irrational anger that drove him to do things he would regret, and even if he wasn't at the stage just yet where he was prepared to do something stupid, I knew that moment was fast approaching. I had to say the right things. I had to deal with this properly.

'Don't speak like that,' I begged of him. 'Calm down, Stuart. Tell me what's happened. Have you seen her? Have you seen Vicky?'

'*No I fucking haven't!*' he screamed.

I heard something crash in the background – I don't know what – and his breathing was heavy, almost panicked.

'Stuart! Talk to me! If you don't talk to me I'm hanging up the phone now.'

That got him speaking. 'I called her up,' he raged, 'to check everything was all right. She answered in her posh voice because her mum was in the room, and said, "Oh, sorry, Stuart, we've decided to have a barbecue in the garden today. Maybe another weekend." '

A barbecue. I looked up to the perfect blue sky and cursed the wonderful weather. I didn't know what to say. I felt so badly for my brother; but at the same time I knew the truth was that this was a situation of his own making. If he hadn't acted so badly in the past, it would never have happened.

'Listen, Stu,' I said, struggling to find something to say that would mollify him, 'I'm sure Vicky's very upset too . . .'

But my words fell on deaf ears as he started getting angry with me, shouting in a way I had never heard before. I fell silent, unused to being spoken to in such a fashion by my brother.

'Just call her, Jayne,' he instructed. 'Tell her to sort it out. She can put a stop to this right now if she wants to.' He hung up.

Suddenly my mind was ablaze with confusion. With

trembling hands I called Vicky but her phone went straight into voicemail, so I tried to calm myself by making a cup of tea, smoking a cigarette and thinking things through. *She can put a stop to this right now if she wants to*. Stuart's words echoed in my head, ominous and dangerous.

I had to speak to Vicky. I tried to call her again. Nothing.

They were not the sort of words that you wanted to hear coming from Stuart's mouth. What had he meant? What did he have in his mind? Something horrible. A petty but brutal campaign of intimidation, no doubt. He would antagonise her, stalk her, do everything in his power to make her life a misery.

I tried Vicky's number yet again. Still nothing.

In many ways my brother was like a child, but instead of throwing tantrums to get his own way, he would bully people, because he knew it got results. I envisaged him knocking on her door and giving her verbal abuse; I envisaged him damaging her car; I envisaged him turning up like a bad penny whenever she least expected it. Poor Vicky would be terrorised. I could barely imagine someone wanting to do that to my beautiful Vicky, least of all someone I loved; but I didn't know what I would be able to do to stop it.

I decided to keep trying to call Vicky, to warn her that he might be coming round. Time after time I dialled her number, but she had clearly turned her phone off and I couldn't get through.

Unease nagging at me, I walked outside into the sunshine. The kids were playing happily, oblivious to the drama that was unfolding elsewhere. My neighbour was outside too, and could clearly tell that something was wrong. Briefly I explained what was happening, then said that I was going to ignore any phone calls for a while. I think something had snapped inside me – all of a sudden I was fed up with being a mediator between these two people who could not sort their problems out on their own. Now I was angry that their issues were spoiling my perfect family day. Perhaps I was being foolish or selfish, but I was mentally exhausted at the time – I felt like a punch-bag, there for Stuart to take his anger out on. Ruefully I told my neighbour that he and Vicky had asked me any number of times to move my family nearer to them in Highmoor Cross. 'I haven't,' I said, 'because it would drive me mad.'

Now, how I wish I could turn the clock back. How I wish I could have been there to calm him down. To prevent what happened next.

But I can't. Simon agreed with me, telling me that just for once I should put Stuart from my mind and try to enjoy our family day together. I knew he was right. I smiled at him and did my best to do what he suggested.

A little while later, however, Stuart called again and I answered the phone this time, albeit with great reluctance. He was still raving. 'Have you spoken to her?' he shouted. 'Is she letting me see her or what?'

I tried to stay calm. 'I haven't spoken to her yet, Stu,' I told him. 'Her phone's been switched off . . .'

My words didn't seem to register, but suddenly I heard tears in his voice. 'I need to see her, Jayne!' he sobbed.

'Stu, you're going to have to be patient.'

I think it was the worst thing I could have said.

'Fuck it!' he shouted. 'Fuck it! I don't want to be patient. You don't jest with a broken man, Jayne.'

'Stuart—'

'*You don't jest with a broken man!*' he repeated. 'Well, if I can't be there, her mother shouldn't fucking be there either. I'm gone. Don't phone me.'

And he hung up once again.

He had told me not to phone him, but I couldn't obey. I rang him straight back. Even in the intervening seconds his voice had changed beyond recognition. He was a mess, full of hurt and rage and madness.

'Don't go round to Vicky's,' I told him firmly. 'It's not fair. Wait until tempers have calmed down.'

He breathed deeply down the phone, as though trying to gain mastery of emotions he didn't understand and could not control. 'I can't stop hurting, Jayne,' he said through clenched teeth. 'I feel as though my heart is being ripped out of my chest. I have to talk to Vicky, Jayne. *I have to talk to her!'*

I closed my eyes – I knew that I was not going to be able to stop him. He was determined. 'Just stay calm, Stu,' I replied. 'That's all I ask. And stay in touch. Please.'

His phone clicked off.

A whirlwind of emotions raged through my mind. I found myself worrying for Vicky and her mum; I found myself worrying for Stuart; if I'm honest, and selfish though it sounds, I found myself worrying for me and my family. If Stuart did something stupid like go round to the house and break the injunction keeping him away, no doubt he would want to use my house as a bail address if he was arrested. The madness in his voice kept echoing through my head. I loved him, and would do almost anything for him, but I couldn't have him living with me, not in the mental state he was in at that moment.

I kept trying to call Vicky, but her phone remained on answerphone and I felt impotent and helpless, so far away from where everything was happening, unable to help. I was involved in this awful situation, inextricably linked to the crazy, warped relationship my brother had with his wife, but I was not in a position to be useful. I wondered if I should call the police, but what could I tell them? I had no idea what was going on and it would only make the situation worse. Stuart and Vicky would sort it out, I reasoned with myself, like they always did.

The shouts of the children playing happily outside suddenly brought me back to my senses. I had my own responsibilities here. It was OK to worry about Stuart and Vicky, I realised, but I couldn't beat myself up about what was going on. It was something they were going to have to sort out for themselves. I repeated that thought in my head several times. *They have to sort this out for themselves. You can't live their lives for them, Jayne.*

Telling myself it was their problem was one thing, putting Stu and Vicky from my mind was quite another, and I continued to fret even as I tried to gain control of myself.

The children started telling me that they were hungry, and so I tried to occupy myself with getting the Sunday lunch ready. Normally it is on the table at two o'clock prompt every Sunday, as regular as clockwork, but today I was late. Riddled with worry, I found it hard to function, but I did not want to let the children know anything was wrong. These were grown-ups' problems: there was no need to stress them out and ruin their lovely day by letting on how worried I was, so I tried to keep up a mask of normality – a difficult thing to do when you are anxious to your very core.

The children lined up at the breakfast bar in our kitchen

as I dished out their dinners for them, before serving a plate up for Simon. Instantly the kids saw there was no plate for me – my appetite had deserted me long ago – and of course the questions started immediately. 'Mum, where's your dinner?' 'Why aren't you eating with us?' 'What's wrong?'

I did my best to smile at them and shrug it off. 'Nothing's wrong, guys,' I lied. 'Mummy's just tired and doesn't feel like eating. Don't worry.' The words sounded hollow in my mouth, and the looks on the faces of my children told me that they didn't believe what I had just said. I could do no more to reassure them, however – the very thought of food made me feel sick.

They looked up at Simon. 'It's OK,' he told them kindly. 'Everything's fine. Eat your dinner before it gets cold.'

I looked around me. By now, on an ordinary Sunday, I would already have washed up all the pots and pans so that I could sit down and enjoy lunch with my family. Today the kitchen looked like a bombsite, with greasy roasting tins and saucepans piled high in the sink, and I was unable even to consider clearing up. I sat with them at the table, my mind only half concentrating on their chatter. Now and then I would stand up to look out of the window, biting on my fingernails until there was nothing left to chew, apart from the flesh surrounding my tattered nails.

All the while, I couldn't stop thinking about Stuart's words of earlier that day. *She can put a stop to this right now if she wants to.* I knew full well that if he went round to the marital home that day there would be an almighty scene; I knew the chances were high that poor Vicky would have to endure a period of Stuart's vindictive bullying; but I comforted myself that it was unlikely to go further than that. After all, Stuart still loved Vicky, didn't he? He had said so enough times in his moments of clarity. He wouldn't do anything to hurt her – not *really* hurt her.

I kept telling myself this. I kept telling myself that it would fizzle out like any number of their tear-ups in the past. But I don't know whether I really believed that. I don't know what I believed. I was too confused and upset.

Normally I don't allow my children to go outside to play immediately after they have eaten, preferring for them to digest their meal before starting to race around again. That day was different: as soon as they had finished their lunch, I told them they could go out into the sunshine again. They were excited by this, but they could tell it was unusual. Luke even made a joke out of it. 'Oh, Mummy must have things on her mind if she's letting us back out. Never mind, at least we get to go out to play!'

We all laughed – the children with real humour, me somewhat half-heartedly.

It was the last time I was to laugh that day. It was the last time I was to laugh for weeks, even months, to follow. Because at half-past three, the phone rang again.

It was Stuart.

'Jayne! Jayne! Is that you?'

'Yes, it's me. What's the matter?'

*'Jayne! Is that you?'*

'Stuart! What's the matter?' There was something in his voice that sent a paralysing shock of sickness into my stomach. I felt my limbs go weak.

Something was wrong. Something was dreadfully, dreadfully wrong.

'What's the matter?' I repeated weakly.

He was out of breath. 'There's police everywhere, Jayne.'

'Police? What are you talking about? What's wrong, Stuart?'

I couldn't get any sense out of him. 'Oh my God, Jayne! You've got to help me.' Desperation and panic dripped from his voice.

'What's going on?' I begged him.

'This can't be happening!' Stuart wailed. *'This can't be happening! No!'*

He started panting again, as though he was running from something.

'You've got to forgive me, Jayne. I'm so fucking sorry. You've got to forgive me. I love you so much, and I always will, but you've got to forgive me.'

'What's happened, Stuart?' I whimpered. But he continued to talk in riddles.

'My God, Jayne, please don't hate me. Please don't hate me. *I can't live any more!*'

'Stuart, I can't help you if I don't know what's happened.'

Maybe he heard me, maybe he didn't. I couldn't tell because he had hung up.

I burst into tears, desperate to know what was happening. I tearfully told a worried Simon what Stuart had said, before punching Vicky's number into my phone, but there was still no answer and I shook it in frustration at not being able to get through to her.

And then Stuart called again. Before he even spoke I could hear horrible cracking thuds as he hit the handset against his head. 'I love you, Vicky!' he screamed. 'I fucking love you so much. I love you and I'm sorry. Why didn't you stop that fucking woman?'

'Who, Stu?' I cried. 'Who? I'm frightened, Stu. Help me understand. Tell me what's happened. You're scaring me.'

But he just shouted again, as though he were in genuine physical pain. '*I must die!*' he yelled, and he sounded as if he meant it. '*I must die!*' he repeated. And again: '*I must die!*'

'Why? What have you done? Come on, Stu, nothing's that bad—'

'I have to take my life. I have to.'

It is difficult to find the words to express how I felt. Stuart sounded so different, and I had no idea of where he was or why he was talking about killing himself. He sounded genuinely petrified. I think that was what shocked me the most. Never in his life, ever since he was a little boy, had I heard him sound scared. Angry, yes. Violent, certainly. But never scared. It wasn't an emotion he ever allowed himself to feel. But the person I was talking to now sounded like someone I didn't even know. A stranger. For a crazy moment I even found myself questioning whether it was him – perhaps this was some sort of sick practical joke. I soon put that thought from my mind, however, when he started talking about taking his life again.

'You can't take your own life, Stu,' I wept. 'You can't. You and Vicky are all I've got, and you just can't.'

'But I can't live without Vicky. I can't. I won't. I have to die.'

Once more, my brother hung up. I fell to the ground in the hallway, his words reverberating in my head like the aftershock of some terrible bell. *I can't live without Vicky. I can't live without Vicky*.

'Where is she?' I wept. 'Where's Vicky?'

But there was nobody there to answer my question.

The unknown horror of that afternoon is a moment that will be with me until the day I die.

I will never forget the dry-mouthed, gut-wrenching anxiety; I will never forget the sense of unreality, as though

I was a helpless actor in somebody else's nightmare. I could not put a name to my terror, I could not say what it was that my brother had done, but I knew something unspeakable had happened. Stuart might have been speaking in riddles, but I knew him well enough to understand that his confused words hid something terrible. I had heard the fear in his voice, and if there was one thing I could recognise, it was fear.

When Stuart called again his voice was, if anything, more manic than before. 'Please forgive me,' he begged. 'Please forgive me, Jayne. I'm so sorry for what I've done.'

Tearfully I continued to try to get him to elaborate, to tell me what had happened; to confide in me, as he always had. But there was nothing I could do to draw the truth out of him. He simply continued to rave: 'It's too late, Jayne. You can't help me any more. It's over.'

'*What have you done, Stuart?*'

'I can't tell you Jayne. You'll never forgive me. *You'll never, ever forgive me.*'

Yet again I tried to call Vicky, but without success. I couldn't understand why I was unable to get in touch with her – if she was in trouble, I wanted to help. In a panic I phoned my sister.

'Mandy,' I urged breathlessly. 'Stuart's in trouble. I don't know what it is, but I think it might be serious. Do you know where Mum and Dad are?'

'I'm with them now,' she said. I didn't think to ask where. By now, my parents had taken to moving around a lot, working for a couple of weeks in one pub before going on to somewhere else.

'Get them to ring him,' I begged Mandy. 'Maybe they can make sense of what's going on. And ring him yourself. Help me find out what's happening.' I think Mandy must have heard the blind panic in my voice: she did exactly as I asked.

From that moment, the calls started coming thick and fast, like a constant, bruising barrage of woe. Mandy called, my parents called, and of course Stuart called. None of them made any more sense than the others – their calls merely served to make the rising wave of panic swell even more than it had before. Occasionally Simon would answer Stuart's calls, but my brother always wanted to talk to me, so Simon would hand the receiver over with a grim look on his face. Amid all the panic, I stood in the kitchen, children playing around me, the chaos in the sink mirroring the chaos in my mind, and I tried, with all my heart, to extract some small strand of sense about what had happened.

Stuart had asked me to forgive him. Why had he said that? What had he done? I knew it had to be terrible, otherwise he would never have said such a thing. Ghastly scenarios stacked up in my head. Had he hit Vicky? Had he hurt her badly? Had he smashed her car or her home? Had he gone for her mum, hurt her, put her in hospital even? It would explain why he was panicking. The one thing Stuart didn't want to do was go back to prison again, and if his temper had got the better of him, with his record and his past that could have been a very real possibility.

At no stage, however, did I even entertain the reality of what had happened.

It seemed barely credible to me that the phone calls from Stuart could get any worse; but when I heard from him at the end of the afternoon it was even more distressing. The phone call started out like all the others. He begged my forgiveness; he told me he loved me; I heard beating sounds that made it quite clear that he was hurting himself in some way. 'I have to suffer like I've made others suffer,' he told me. 'I want you to understand. I *need* you to understand. I'm sorry I've been such a burden to you over the years, Jayne, but the time has come for me to die.'

'You haven't been a burden to me, Stu,' I replied weakly. 'You've never been a burden—'

As I spoke, however, I heard him take a deep breath. There was a silence between us, and even without hearing him say a word I could sense somehow that a calm had descended upon him.

'What's wrong, Stu?' I whispered.

'I can't stand the fact that I let you down,' he said quietly. Instantly I knew what he was talking about. He was not speaking about the day's events, whatever they may have been; he was speaking about the past. About Graham.

'It has to be dealt with,' he insisted, his voice flat and monotone. Determined. 'It has to be dealt with now. Once and for all.'

'Please, Stuart,' I breathed, terrified by what he was saying. 'Please stop talking like this.'

Suddenly he snapped and was back to his old self. 'It's not right!' he shouted. 'It's not right the way you suffered. I'm going there now to put an end to it. I've got nothing to lose. And when it's done, then I'm going to die.'

I felt trapped by my pain. Was this what it was all about? 'Please, Stuart,' I begged him, 'we've been through this. Please don't do anything to him.'

'I can't stand that I let you down!' he repeated with a roar.

'Don't keep punishing yourself like this, Stuart. It's not your fault.' Everything seemed surreal as I quickly tried to think of things to say to him, things that would bring him back to normality, to sanity – or as near to sanity as it was possible for him to be. 'It's wrong of you to take your life without saying goodbye to Mum and Dad.'

He fell silent. After a few seconds I heard muffled sobbing, followed by a half-hearted, 'Yeah.' It sounded as though I was too late; it sounded as though he was too far down the path he had set himself.

'Stuart!' I yelled. 'Are you OK? Stuart! Please don't do this to me! Talk to me! *Stuart!*'

But there was no reply. He had hung up yet again.

I sat down – deciding if I should call the police or not. I just didn't know what to do or what was going on, but I knew I had to do something. Things felt totally out of control and I was scared senseless. The television in the corner of the front room was on, the volume low as it quietly bathed the room in its flickering light. I hadn't really noticed it in all the confusion, and was oblivious to its meaningless burble, just white noise in the background. I paced the house, still chewing at my tattered fingernails, fidgeting and unable to stay still. I wanted to do something, anything, to help, but I didn't know what. Trying to fill my time, I went about the business of getting the kids' school clothes ready for the following morning. Half-heartedly I considered doing some cleaning. How Stuart would have laughed at me, trying to focus my mind on the housework at a time like this. But I needed something to distract me. Should I take the sofa covers off to clean them? Should I tackle the washing up? In the end I couldn't motivate myself to do anything.

Outside it was still warm and sunny, but none of the warmth of that day seemed to break through the chill that surrounded me. I wandered into the front room for the hundredth time that day and perched on the edge of the sofa. My eyes were fixed on the television screen. It was tuned to a news channel, but I did not really take any of it in.

Until, that is, I saw something I recognised.

It was footage of Highmoor Cross, the village in Oxfordshire where Stuart and Vicky lived.

Like a diver coming up to the surface for air, my internalised worries faded away and I concentrated on nothing but the picture in front of me.

There were reporters and police and cordons.

And then I saw it. A single word, emblazoned across the television screen. A small word, but ominous and dreadful to see.

It said, quite simply, 'Murder'.

# 13

## The Policeman in the Attic

Murder.

You see it on the television all the time, and you feel sorry for the victims and the families involved. But it never quite hits home; the word never quite strikes you a blow in the pit of your stomach. Why should it? Murder is something that always happens to other people.

Perhaps that was why I could not bring myself to believe it. It was a mistake, a coincidence. I persuaded myself that there were any number of explanations for what I was watching on the television. This had nothing to do with what had been going on today. But still, Simon and I could not tear our eyes away from the screen.

The phone rang. It startled me, and I scrambled to pick it up. I heard Mandy's voice, full of panic, at the other end. 'Jayne!' she shouted. 'You watching the television? If not, you'd better switch it on.'

'Yeah, I'm watching it,' I replied, nausea rising through my body.

We fell silent, neither knowing what to say to the other.

I could hear the same news programme that I was watching echo over the phone line as we remained stunned, bewildered and speechless. Finally we both spoke at the same time. 'I'll call you back,' we said in unison.

I went on staring at the television.

Time seemed to stand still. I was consumed with shock as my head played out the possibilities that it might be Stu. I remembered the argument that he and Vicky had had about the gun he had acquired. What had he said? That it was just for shooting pigeons. He wouldn't be so stupid as to—

I halted that line of thought. It wasn't true. It *couldn't* be true.

The phone rang again. It was Stuart.

He was raving, just like before. I couldn't bring myself to ask the question I so needed an answer to, so I found myself tiptoeing around him. 'Please tell me where Vicky is,' I cried.

He refused to answer.

'Stuart,' I whispered, my eyes still fixed on the television. 'I don't want to talk to you any more if you won't tell me what's happening.'

'Don't do this to me, Jayne!' he roared. 'I need you. I need you more than ever. Please don't let me down.'

His words were like arrows in my heart. In that moment, a scene from my childhood flashed before my eyes. I was sitting, frightened and alone, on a hard wooden floor scared of the dark. And then he was there, Stuart, putting his arm around me, holding me tight, telling me that everything was going to be all right.

He had always been there for me. Despite everything, he had always been there. Now he was asking the same of me, and it twisted me up inside that I did not know if I could give him what he wanted.

'Why are police everywhere, Stuart?' I asked quietly.

'They're after me. I know they're after me.' And then those words again. 'I can't live without Vicky. I've got to die.' He hung up again as I buried my face in my hands and wept. I heard the chatter of my children playing outside in the sunshine, and I was thankful that they hadn't come back inside to see me in this dreadful state.

I don't know how long it was until the next newsflash came up on the television, but I remember watching it through a visor of tears. 'Police have surrounded the Highmoor Cross area of Oxfordshire and are looking for a man in his late thirties armed with a gun. If you see this man, call the police immediately. Do not approach him, as he is believed to be highly dangerous.'

I saw the words 'Triple shooting' emblazoned across the screen. And then the words that I will never forget: 'One dead, two critical.'

I grabbed the TV remote and frantically started flicking

through the channels in the hope that I might be able to glean more news from somewhere else. I was hysterical. All I wanted to know was that Vicky and her mum were all right, that the shootings I was learning about on the news were nothing to do with my brother. But I couldn't find anything to confirm or deny what I wanted – what I *needed* – to know.

Until, that is, there was another newsflash.

They had a name for the armed, dangerous man the police were hunting in the village of Highmoor Cross, and the name was now flashing across my screen.

It was Stuart Horgan.

It's strange how your intuition can play tricks on you. I saw the words on the screen; I pieced together the jigsaw in my head; and yet I still refused to believe what was so obviously true. It was just a name. Lots of people have the same name, and there could easily be two Stuart Horgans in Highmoor Cross. There could easily still be an explanation.

'It's not him,' I whispered to Simon, though whether I was trying to persuade him or myself I couldn't say. He didn't respond either way.

Stuart rang again and again. One minute he would be crying, the next he would be calm. For myself, I felt a dreadful numbness fall over my body. I was too scared to ask him outright if Vicky had been shot; I was too much of a coward to learn whether or not he was capable of such a terrible act. As time went on, I found I could not even speak to him.

He called out my name several times: 'Jayne, please talk to me. *Please*. You're all I have . . .' I could do nothing but cry down the phone in response; now it was me hanging up on him. I wished I had some way of getting hold of Vicky, but her phone remained unobtainable and I had no phone numbers for any of her family.

The conversations did nothing for my confidence that the Stuart Horgan on the news was not my brother. I collapsed on to the sofa, head in my hands, and tried to straighten out my thoughts. What should I do? What was the right thing? First of all, I needed to establish to my own satisfaction that this wasn't *my* Stuart. There was only one way I was going to be able to do this, and that was by phoning the police and trying to find out. If I did that, though, and if it was my brother that the police were after, surely I would only be making his perilous situation worse.

I hesitated. And then I thought of what he had said. 'I can't live without Vicky.' I thought of her smiling face, her adorable nature. I thought of her as my friend – as my sister, almost – and the now familiar feeling of dread hit me in the stomach. If something had happened to this woman whom I loved so much, I couldn't bear it; and if something had happened to her at Stuart's hand, then my duty was clear. It didn't matter that he was my brother; it didn't matter that he had looked after me and cared for me; nothing else mattered at all.

If he had hurt Vicky, he had to be stopped.

Violence was not the answer to his problems or mine. The Stuart who was out there on the run was not the same Stuart who had looked after me as a child. He had changed. If he had done what the television was accusing him of, he had become a monster. You can't protect someone like that. You can't hide him. You can't let him carry on doing what he's doing.

I picked up the telephone and called the police.

I explained my situation: that I'd had Stuart on the phone several times and he was sounding very upset; that I had just seen the news.

'Who are you?' the voice at the other end asked.

'Stuart's sister,' I explained.

I was put through to a different section – the Silver Command unit – where I tried to explain to them everything I knew. 'I'm Vicky Horgan's sister-in-law,' I told them. 'I just want to know that she's all right.'

They took my name and number, but didn't give me any information about what was going on. Instead they asked me if I had heard from my brother.

'Yes,' I said, and I told them about the calls I had received.

'But please, just tell me if Vicky is all right.'

Again they declined to give me any information. 'We'll call you back,' they told me.

And so I went back to the agonising business of waiting.

Stuart's phone calls continued. They were becoming shorter and shorter, more and more manic. One time he would be hitting his head against the handset; another he would be yelling that he had to die; another he would be telling me how much he loved me. But he was deteriorating – that much was clear. At one point he became suddenly silent in the middle of a phone call and I honestly believed he had killed himself. I felt myself go weak with horror; but then he called again, and to hear his incoherent rant was almost a relief.

Evening came. To me, it felt more like the middle of the night, the afternoon had appeared to stretch on so long. I called the kids in and told them they would have to go to bed early. They were as good as gold – clearly they must have sensed something was wrong – but terrible as it sounds I knew I could not deal with having to hide the events of the day from them along with everything else. I was still confused and in the dark, and I didn't want them to see or hear anything until I knew in my mind exactly what was going on.

Simon and I settled anxiously down in front of the television, our sole source of news as we waited for the police to call me back and let me know what was happening. As the tragedy unfolded tortuously in front of my eyes, I was barraged with information that I did not want to believe but could not stop myself taking in. One dead and two critical, they kept telling me. One dead and two critical.

And then, a little later, two dead.

I still had half my mind trying to persuade myself that there was a perfectly logical explanation; but by now common sense was also starting to kick in, and the other half of me became suffused with the awful realisation that Stuart had gone too far this time. I couldn't help him any more.

I'm ashamed to admit it, but as I sat there, selfish thoughts about my own predicament started creeping into my head. How was I going to manage without the two people in the world I loved so very much? I prayed that one of the dead was not Vicky, because I couldn't imagine my life without her. If what I feared was true, Stuart was going to go to prison for the rest of his life. Either that, or he was going to die. Somehow, I found myself reconciled to those ideas, but the one thing I could not face was the prospect of losing Vicky. I needed to get to her and give her a hug, and the fact that I could not do that started to drive me to distraction.

Ten o'clock. The police had still not called me back, and all I had to go on was the sketchy information from the television. I could do nothing but pace the house, totally out of my mind and contorted with worry. Simon and I tried to derive some sort of comfort from the silence – the fact that I hadn't heard from them was surely some kind of indication that Stuart wasn't implicated in all this. After all, they had heard from me hours ago. But even as I thought that, I knew I was clutching at straws.

Outside, all was still. It had remained warm. The children were all asleep upstairs, but it was unnaturally quiet, even for a Sunday evening. Ominously quiet. Almost on autopilot I walked out of the front room on my way to the kitchen in order to make myself a cup of tea. But when I reached the hallway, I stopped.

There was a silhouette at the door.

'Simon!' I called, under my breath.

He joined me in the corridor. The silhouette was still there; I could see the head bobbing around. Whoever it was was moving.

'Someone's here,' he breathed.

We stood there, frozen, for what seemed like an age.

'I should open the door,' I whispered.

'No,' he told me. 'Just wait. We don't know who it is. See what happens.'

I shook my head. 'I can't just stand here,' I said. We exchanged a long look, and then I walked to the door. I took a deep breath to calm my shaking nerves, and then I opened it.

When I saw what was on my doorstep, I screamed and fell to my knees.

Five or six people were waiting for me. One of them held a heavy metal battering ram and had just moved it back over his shoulder ready to break the door down. All of them looked shocked – they hadn't knocked at the door, so they clearly weren't expecting it to be opened, and I could instantly tell that it wasn't a good idea to give these people surprises. I saw flat caps and black bullet-proof jackets. I saw guns, small ones but somehow all the more vicious-looking for that.

*'He's not here!'* I yelled. *'Please, he's not here. I haven't done anything wrong.'*

I looked up at them. Beyond the police officers on my doorstep, there were perhaps another ten of them in the road. They all wore black body armour and black helmets, and had weapons pointing in my direction. All of a sudden I became aware of the little red marks of their laser sights dotted all around the entrance to my house.

No one said a word, and in that moment I thought I was going to die.

I heard Simon's voice behind me, but before I could even work out what he was saying, I felt strong arms grabbing me roughly: two officers, a man and a large woman, had grabbed me by my arms and were dragging me out on to the street. 'Stuart's not here!' I heard myself screaming.

'I don't know where he is!' But they didn't reply, and continued to march me with grim and unrelenting determination down the street.

The cold hand of panic seized my heart. Simon was shouting in the background, 'My kids are asleep! *My kids are asleep!*' and everything seemed like it had suddenly been plunged into mayhem. I could still see officers with guns all around me, and I remember thinking to myself that this is how people get shot by accident. If something went wrong when they went into the children's bedroom – well, it did not bear thinking about.

I started to whimper. 'Let me go to my kids. Please don't go barging in there.' But my words went unheard as they continued to walk me along the street. I became vaguely aware of the neighbours opening their doors and putting their heads out of the windows.

'*Get inside!*' the police officers started shouting. '*Get inside and shut your windows. Now!*'

The faces of my children popped into my head, and I honestly wondered if I had seen them for the last time. I knew that innocent people had been killed earlier that day. Was I going to be next? Why did they keep pointing the guns in my direction? What did they think I had done? My kids are asleep, I thought to myself. I love them and I don't want to die.

These jumbled, terrified thoughts zapped around in my

brain. Through my tears, it became clear that the two officers who were holding me so firmly were taking me towards a police van at the end of the street. I focused on it with all my might. If I could just get there, I would be safe. Accidents couldn't happen inside the van, could they?

At last we made it to the vehicle. I was lifted up and placed in the back.

I sat down and noticed that some kind of video recorder was pointed at me, recording anything I had to say. I was a trembling mess, my teeth chattering uncontrollably with the fear, and my body shaking. I wept and I shivered.

As I sat in the van, the big woman who had grabbed me so forcibly started speaking. 'Jayne!' she said harshly. 'Where's Stuart? Have you seen Stuart?'

I shook my head; perhaps she couldn't tell that I had done so because my body was shaking so much anyway.

And then she spoke again. Even now, the words that came from her mouth seem unbelievable, like something said by a shadowy character in a nightmare of unknowable terror.

'Listen to me, Jayne,' she said, her voice urgent and serious. 'Stuart has shot and killed Vicky. He has shot and killed her sister, Emma. Their mother is in hospital fighting for her life. So if you know where he is, you have got to tell me. And now.'

*

*Back in the house, all is chaos. Simon has begged the police to let him wake the children up himself, but they have their reasons for doing things their own way and they refuse to allow this. The children wake up to find men with guns in their bedroom. To my eternal pride, they remain calm, though Luke will later tell me that he was terrified for his life. When the armed police storm into his room, he thinks they are going to kill him. Once they have secured the room, however, one of the officers smiles at him. 'Go into your sisters' room,' he tells him. 'You can watch a video, but don't tell your mum and dad that you're staying up too late . . .' Luke understands that he is making a little joke with him, to take the strain out of such a traumatic experience. He realises that the policemen are probably not going to kill them.*

*Once all the kids are safely in the same room, they stand anxiously at the doorway watching what is going on. The police officers open up the hatch to the loft: one of them climbs up into the loft while another urges the children back into the bedroom away from the door. Poor little Alyce, who is only four, does not have the opportunity to see the policeman come back out. To this day she thinks there is a man with a gun in our loft, and that he could come out at any time. It scares her nightly.*

'No!' I whispered. The information that the policewoman had so calmly conveyed to me refused to sink in. I suddenly seemed to have no control over my body whatsoever. My limbs started to shake.

'Where is he, Jayne?'

'*No!*'

'Has your brother been in touch?'

I tried to breathe, but the air didn't seem to fill my lungs.

'What did he say to you, Jayne? Did you know he was going to kill them?'

'*No, no, no!*' I screamed, breaking down.

She kept firing questions as floods of tears continued to wave over me. I couldn't answer any of them, as my tears overcame any words I tried to say. 'I'm sorry,' I managed finally. 'I'm so sorry. I'm so sorry for crying.'

The policewoman stretched out her arm and held my hand. 'It's all right,' she said with some compassion, 'I know it's a shock. But you do understand that we have to ask you questions, Jayne?'

I tried to compose myself. Despite the warmth of the evening, I felt freezing cold – the shock, I suppose – and I could not get out of my mind the image of Vicky's body, cold and lifeless, lying where she had fallen by Stuart's hand.

Why did she have to die?

How could my brother have done such a thing?

I shook my head in numb incomprehension as the stark realisation of what had happened started to hit home. My life had been destroyed once before, many years ago. I had rebuilt it and become strong. Now, along with the lives of so many other people, it had been destroyed once more, thanks to the actions of my brother.

'Listen to me, Jayne,' the policewoman said. 'We know you were close to your brother. We think he might come here. We think he might come after you. We want to put you under witness protection.'

The world seemed to spin.

Would he really come and harm me?

How could somebody I loved so much have committed such evil?

How could the lives of decent people have been extinguished with such ease?

How were any of us going to cope with what had happened?

I looked up at the policewoman, who had continued to stare implacably, waiting for some sort of response. It was suddenly clear to me what I had to do, for whom I had to be strong. I took a deep, shaky breath and mustered the strength to speak.

'I want to see my children,' I said.

# 14
## *Birdsong*

How do you tell your children that their uncle is a murderer? How do you explain that the same man who held them on his lap when they were born, the man who read them stories and took them to the park and showered them with love and kindness, is a killer? How do you find the words? As I was led back into the house under the watchful eyes of the armed police officers who still clearly viewed me with suspicion, I tried to formulate some kind of explanation to give them. But the words did not come.

I walked into the house. All our telephones and mobiles were piled on the kitchen table so that we couldn't use them, but making phone calls was the last thing on my mind at that moment. I just wanted to see my children, so I hurried up to the bedroom. Emma, my eldest, was still out with her friends, but the three little ones were sitting there on a bed, as good as gold, their angelic little faces looking up at me with such fear and confusion. They were holding back their tears, as though they didn't want to upset me any more than I already was; but I could see that they also wanted their mother to give them some sort of explanation, to tell them that everything was going to be all right. It broke my heart that I was not going to be able to do that.

Luke was holding on tightly to his sisters, as though it was the last time he would ever be able to do so. He was the first to speak, his voice cracked as he asked the question that had clearly been on all their minds from the moment they saw men with guns in their bedroom.

'Mummy,' his little voice piped up, 'are they going to shoot you?'

His question ripped me to shreds. I bent down to hug them all. 'No, darling,' I said in a voice that was not at all confident. I gathered them in my arms, feeling their warmth and drinking in the smell of their hair. In that moment I remembered acutely the day each of them was born. The sensation – that overwhelming feeling of relief that they were all OK – was the same, and I allowed the very fact of their presence to reassure me just a little bit. Just as my family of dolls had given me some strength during the dark days of my childhood, so my real family helped me through that almost impossible moment.

I knew that the precious silence would not last. I knew that before long they would start asking me questions. Sure enough, they did.

'Are we going to die?' Luke whispered.

'No, darling. You're not going to die.'

'Why are they angry with us? Have we done something bad?'

'It's not your fault,' I whispered, tears coming to my eyes.

'But they have big guns and crash helmets, Mummy. And they went into the loft with lights—'

'They need to speak to Uncle Stuart,' I interrupted him. 'They thought he might be here.'

I started to muster the courage to tell them that their Auntie Vicky was dead. That Uncle Stuart had killed her. But at the last moment my willpower deserted me. They had had enough trauma for one evening; they didn't need any more. And I now realised that I was too weak to deal with it, in any case.

'That's all I know,' I lied. 'The police have a job to do. They just want to make sure we're all safe and that there's nobody in the house that there shouldn't be.'

'Is Uncle Stuart all right, Mum? Is he here?'

'No, Luke,' I replied quietly. 'He's not here.'

'Are they going to kill Uncle Stuart, Mum?'

I shook my tearful head. 'They just want to ask him a few questions,' I whispered. I tried to smile at them. 'You can all sleep in the same room tonight,' I told them. 'I'll come and check on you soon.'

It was so difficult to leave them, but I knew I had to. The police were clearly not convinced that I wasn't helping Stuart in some way, and I doubted it would be long before they came in and removed me from my children. That was not something I wished them to see. As I walked down the stairs, I saw a group of officers talking in whispers: they looked at me suspiciously as I descended, and I was ushered into the kitchen.

The female police officer was waiting for me. She looked serious, and the sympathy she had displayed in the van was now replaced by a no-nonsense attitude. I was told to call Emma and get her home as quickly as possible. My daughter heard the urgency in my voice and said she would come straight back. And then the police questioning started. Perhaps it was my paranoia, but the officer's voice seemed to me to be full of suspicion. I really tried to convince her that we were an ordinary, innocent family, but I suppose it was her job to take nothing on trust. No matter how tired I became, the questions didn't stop coming. Why did Stuart have a gun? What could have driven him to do such a thing? Why had he kept calling me? Did I know where he was? Was I hiding him?

I did my best to reply honestly, but some of these questions I simply didn't know the answer to. The police-woman grew increasingly frustrated with me – it can't have been easy for her, knowing that a dangerous killer was on the loose and suspecting I knew more than I did. She was only doing her job, but that didn't make me feel better at the time.

'You're lying, Jayne,' she told me at one point.

I shook my head. 'I'm not lying. I swear.'

I could tell she didn't believe me. The questions became relentless. They merged into one, and my answers became increasingly tearful and repetitive. The policewoman refused to be satisfied with what I said, and as emotion and exhaustion overcame me, I suppose I became less and less coherent. At one point she banged her fist on the table. 'I'm sick of your lies, Sterne!' she shouted at me.

'*I'm . . . not . . . lying*,' I told her, but it was no good. She still acted as though she believed I was hiding something, and I could do nothing to persuade her. The tension between me and the police mounted.

I became desperate to be of some sort of help, to make them believe that just because Stuart was my brother, I was not like him and I didn't condone what he had done. The policewoman gave me a phone number, and said I had received several calls from that number since they had arrived and confiscated my phone. Did I know who it was? I replied honestly. I said I couldn't be sure, but I thought it might be my parents. I explained that I never really knew their telephone numbers as they never stayed in one place for long enough, but if it was a number outside of London, it was likely to be them.

'Do you think your brother would contact them?' the policewoman asked me.

I thought for a moment and remembered what I had said to Stuart about not killing himself before going to say goodbye to Mum and Dad. Slowly I nodded my head. 'Yes,' I told her. 'I think it's possible.'

I knew, as I spoke, that I might be giving Stuart up. I also knew it was the right thing to do.

The policewoman allowed me a moment to go outside and smoke a cigarette. Armed response officers were still outside with their evil-looking guns, and I stared into the darkness for a while, reliving the events of the day silently in my head. I felt a sense of loss more bitter than I can perhaps make clear, and I knew Stuart had to be brought to justice for his dreadful crime. I finished my cigarette, stubbed it out on the ground and quietly returned into the house. For the first time since the police arrived, the kitchen was empty, and the telephone sat on the kitchen table. Surreptitiously, looking over my shoulder, I picked it up and hit the redial button. Of course, I recognised the voice that answered.

'Mum, is that you?'

'Hello, Jayne,' she said quietly.

I think that was the moment I must have known that Stuart was there.

I stepped outside to where the policewoman was and handed her the phone. 'It's my mum,' I said.

I thought I had done well; I was not prepared for the look of fury that crossed the policewoman's eyes. She grabbed the phone from me and shouted at me to stop playing games. I could hear my mum's voice calling my name down the phone, but I could not answer her as I was being berated by the policewoman. 'If you have put any of my officers at risk, you're nicked!' she shouted.

'I'm sorry,' I cried. 'I'm so sorry. I thought I was doing the right thing. I think he's there!'

The policewoman gave me a look of utter disdain and walked away.

Time passed, excruciatingly slowly – the longest night of my life.

Simon did his best to comfort me, but I was beyond comfort. I felt angry with myself and embarrassed for the mistake I had made, and I could not get the image of Vicky, cold and dead, out of my mind. I wanted to go to her, to hold her hand and keep her warm. Somehow it would have made me feel better, even though I knew that the worst had happened. It just didn't seem right that she should be by herself. I wasn't going to be going anywhere, however. The police saw to that, with their guns and their constant questions.

Half-past three. The policewoman walked into my

kitchen, a broad smile on her face. How can anyone be smiling, I wondered to myself. I soon found out it was a smile of relief.

'It's all right, Jayne Sterne,' she said, 'we've found your brother.'

She said the word 'brother' with such distaste. I wanted to be angry with the woman, but I could not find it in me to blame her. A million questions popped into my head. Was he all right? Where had they found him? But I did not have the energy to ask them.

Everything was so unreal. The police disappeared almost as suddenly as they had arrived, and within only a few minutes the house, which up until then had been milling with armed police officers, was empty. Upstairs the children were asleep. In the front room there was just me, Simon, the silence and an emptiness inside that I thought would never leave me. We sat there together, neither knowing what to say to the other.

'We're going to have to tell the kids,' I said finally to Simon.

He took my hand. 'They already know, Jayne.'

I looked at him quizzically.

'They overheard it all from the police,' he said. 'They're not stupid.'

I nodded numbly. It was all too much to take in. I sat there in silence once more, gazing aimlessly around the house. The place was a mess. My normally immaculate house had scuff marks on the floor from where so many people had been walking around, and every surface in the kitchen was covered with dirty crockery. I felt ashamed with the state of the place, but for the moment I had neither the enthusiasm nor the energy to do anything about it.

I have never known such desolation. Outside of my immediate family, Stuart and Vicky were my life. Now Vicky was dead, along with her sister, and Stuart could never be forgiven for what he had done. It was as though someone had taken my life away from me. It shames me to say it, but in that dark hour not even the thought of my children stopped me from entertaining ideas of suicide. Of joining Vicky. I would be no good to my little ones, now that the very soul had been ripped from me. The worst had happened – worse even than the things that had been inflicted upon me during my childhood – and I felt like I would be no good to my children any more. Part of me had died with Vicky – perhaps it would be best to end it now.

I don't know how long it was that I sat there, those desperate thoughts flitting through my mind. Minutes? Hours? Time seemed to have no meaning any more.

Simon, exhausted, went to bed. After a while I started to wander round the kitchen in a daze, clearing things up, cleaning. It seemed so strange, doing normal things in such an abnormal situation. I continued anyway. Perhaps I thought that by creating order in my house I could create some order in my life, but it was not to be. When the kitchen was clean I just went back to sitting, staring and thinking.

About Vicky. About her smile, and her laughter, and her goodness. It seemed impossible to me that such a vibrant life could have been so suddenly extinguished. Unreal. Perhaps I would wake up soon. Perhaps she would phone me up like she did almost every day and tell me that it was a mistake. A joke. It hadn't happened.

But I wasn't asleep. It wasn't a mistake. It wasn't a joke. This was cold, harsh reality.

I closed my eyes and thought of her face.

Gradually, out of the silence, I became aware of a sound. It was a pretty sound – unnaturally pretty, given the circumstances.

It was birdsong.

Outside was pitch-dark. I had never heard birds singing during the night-time before. Somehow, though, it didn't seem peculiar, because deep within me I persuaded myself that it wasn't birdsong at all. It was Vicky and her sister, letting me know that they were OK. That they had gone to a place far away from the troubles of this world. A place where nobody could harm them ever again.

I stayed up, sitting on the front doorstep and listening to

the birdsong, and watching as the steely grey of dawn imperceptibly lit up the sky.

It was only afterwards that I learned the truth about Stuart's movements on the day of the murders.

He had arrived at the house in Highmoor Cross carrying a .410 single-barrelled shotgun. He jumped over the garden gate, landing close to Vicky, Jacqui and Emma. Immediately, he aimed the gun straight at Jacqui and shot her in the stomach. Vicky ran into the house and Stuart chased her, reloading the gun as he did so. When he caught up with her, he shot her in the head, then returned to the garden where Emma was trying to phone the police on her mobile. Stuart shot Emma in the torso before she could complete the call. Witnesses reported seeing him leave through the front door, still carrying the gun.

Once he had left the house, he got into his car and went straight to the off-licence where he bought several bottles of alcohol. He got back into the car and started driving. I was the first person he called, and by that time he had already started drinking. He drove towards Peterborough, where my parents were working in a pub, drinking all the while. It must have been during this time that he kept phoning me.

Still carrying a loaded gun, Stuart arrived at the pub in Peterborough where my parents and sister were waiting for him. He continued to drink heavily. Then he fell to the ground in front of them and started beating his head against the hard floor, saying, 'I've killed my wife. I've killed my wife.'

They tried to calm him down, and he kept asking them if they still loved him. All the while he continued to drink heavily from a bottle of Southern Comfort. My family found themselves in an impossible situation.

When I called, it became clear to everyone that it was all over, but it was Stuart's decision to give himself up in the end. I suppose he must have known that the police would get him sooner or later. He took the gun, walked to the outside of the pub, put the weapon on the floor and lay down in front of it.

It did not take the police long to surround the area. There were lots of them, with sniffer dogs and body armour, and armed to the back teeth. Stuart came quietly.

He was taken to Loddon Valley Police Station where he admitted having had an argument with his family members. He told police that he had found the gun and ammunition in the woods. He said that when he had jumped over the fence, holding the gun, he had only intended to frighten Vicky, Emma and Jacqui, but that the gun had gone off by accident. It was noted by the police that the gun in question could only be fired once before having to be reloaded. Given that three people had been shot, it would have to have been reloaded twice. He had two other live cartridges in his possession.

Stuart admitted that he had drunk a large amount of alcohol during the day. He also said that on average he drank fifteen pints of lager a day, and several vodkas.

He was subsequently charged with two counts of murder and one of attempted murder.

Having been properly cautioned, he made no reply.

# 15

# *The Final Tragedy*

Daybreak.

When I was a child, the rising of the sun had always made things better. It chased away the shadows. That wasn't going to happen today.

Who would have thought that barely twenty-four hours had passed since I had woken up so light of heart the previous morning? From my doorstep I started to hear the sounds of the city – cars, buses, people making their way to work. For them it was just another ordinary Monday morning. For me, nothing would ever be the same again. The sun had risen on a whole different world that I didn't want to be a part of.

The house was still quiet, its exhausted inhabitants fast asleep. As soon as I knew it was late enough, I slipped away to the local newsagents to buy all the newspapers. It was an uncomfortable walk – I felt as though everybody knew who I was, as though they were all staring at me. But it was going to be another hot, sunny day, so there was no chance of hiding under hats or heavy coats, and I just had to stick it out. As I walked down my street, I felt my eyes flickering towards each window to see if anybody was peering out to look at me. I was smothered with paranoia. Had they seen what had happened on the television? Had they read the papers? Did they know? I almost felt as if it was me who had committed the crime, and I wondered whether the fact that my eyes were so bloodshot with crying would make everybody realise who I was.

I bought the newspapers, but did not read them immediately. I had to get home first. The children would be waking soon, and I needed to be there for them. They were getting up just as I arrived back. On a normal morning, they would run down the stairs excitedly. But today was far from normal. Instead they shouted down, 'Mummy, is that you? Is it safe to come down now, Mummy? Have the gunmen gone?'

I went to the bottom of the staircase and looked up; their frightened little faces stared back down at me. 'It's all right,' I told them. 'It's safe to come down. They've all gone.'

Instantly my children were around me. We sat down at the kitchen table, and I made some sort of attempt at establishing normality by trying to get them to eat breakfast. They didn't seem to be that interested, though, and just picked unenthusiastically at the cereal in their bowls.

It was little Bethany who broke the silence, looking at

me with her beautiful eyes wide. 'Uncle Stuart didn't kill Vicky on purpose, Mum.' She was only young, but she sounded for all the world like she was trying to console me.

'Yes, Bethany. He did.' I spoke with a quiet determination, as though I was trying to persuade myself as well as her.

She shook her head. 'No, Mum. That's not what happened. They were having a barbecue, and Uncle Stuart had a gun so that he could shoot a rabbit for their dinner, but the bullet went through the rabbit and into Vicky by mistake.'

Nothing I could say would disabuse my daughter of her firm conviction, and to this day she wholly believes that this is what happened. I could do nothing but hug her and hold her tight.

Luke sat at the table, his eyes a mystery. He didn't say much, but asked if he could get ready for school. He sounded angry and it was clear to me how much he was hurting.

As he walked out of the kitchen, I left with him. 'Do you want to talk?' I asked.

For a moment he hesitated. Then he turned round and cuddled me. 'I was afraid I wasn't going to see you again,' he said. 'I'm so happy you're here, Mum.'

As for Alyce, the youngest, she didn't speak about the night before over breakfast; but when the time came for us to go back upstairs again, she asked me to go up with her. She believed there were still men in the loft, and so Simon and I had to get the loft ladder down and let each of the children look up there to see that they had all gone. Alyce remained unconvinced, however.

My brave children got ready for school that day as per usual. Simon and I were nervous about letting them go, but decided in the end that school was as safe a place as anywhere else. As we left, they had only one request: 'Will you find out how Uncle Stuart is, Mum? We want to know that he's OK.' I felt so proud of them as I waved them into their classrooms before going back home to read what the papers had been saying.

Reading the news that morning was a sickening experience. They had dubbed my brother the Barbecue Murderer, and lurid stories of what he had done were bannered across the pages of every paper. They all told the same horrific tale, illustrated with pictures of Vicky's garden where the shooting had taken place. There were photographs, too, of Stuart and the victims. I was referred to as 'the sister'. My eyes scanned over the newsprint as I desperately tried to glean some new information about what had gone on the previous day, but there was nothing there I didn't know already. What shocked me, however, was the huge level of interest in my brother. I suppose that was only natural, but when you aren't used to seeing your family in the papers, it comes as a surprise, no matter what they have done. I suddenly realised how remiss I had been in not warning my children's school about the events of the previous day. Of course they needed to know, and I steeled myself to phone the headmistress and confess to her that I was the sister of the notorious killer. I felt the cold hand of humiliation brush over me as I reached for the phone and started to dial the number.

I had not yet finished dialling, however, when there was a knock on the door. I couldn't think who it could be, but I put the phone down anyway and went to answer it. There was a man there whom I did not recognise. He wore a suit and a wide smile.

'Jayne Sterne?' he asked.

'Yes,' I replied, a bit nervously. 'Can I help you?'

'I'm so sorry to bother you at this difficult time,' he replied. 'I'm a journalist, and I understand you are the sister of Stuart Horgan. I wonder if you would like to tell his side of the story.'

I blinked at him, slightly stunned. When I did speak, it was in a weak, cracked voice. 'I'm sorry,' I said. 'I can't talk to you. I . . . I've got nothing to say.'

'There are always two sides to every story,' he tried to persuade me.

I shook my head. 'No.' I could feel my voice wavering. 'I'm sorry. I just want to be left alone.' I shut the door and pressed my back against the wall as I struggled to master a wave of panic. A chill descended over my body, and I started to shake. How had he found me so quickly? Terrible thoughts started entering my head: if he had found me with such ease, what if other people wanted to find me? What if someone read about the murders and wanted retribution? What if they wanted Stuart's family to suffer the way Vicky's family were suffering?

Blinded by this sudden and all-pervasive paranoia, I became overwhelmed with an unreasonable need to hide myself: running upstairs I started looking manically around for a place to conceal myself. But it was a moment of madness, and of course there was nowhere to hide.

That was the first time I had a journalist knock on my door, but it was by no means the last. In the days that followed, my family and I were subjected to a torrent of impeccably polite but ruthlessly persistent journalists doorstepping us and following us in the street. All they wanted to talk about was Stuart – they rarely mentioned Vicky, as if she had never even existed, which upset me more than anything – but I continued to refuse to speak to anyone. It wasn't just that I feared I wouldn't be able to stay calm if I was forced to speak to them; if I'm honest I would have to say that I felt ashamed. Any normal person would want to be in the newspapers for a good reason – a great achievement or as a character in a happy story – but not this. The journalists had a job to do, though, I suppose. They didn't care that my family and I found their intrusions upsetting, but they continued to hound us.

My children had their own victimisations to deal with, worse in their way. Goading from unkind schoolmates; graffiti on the walls saying that they were part of a family of murderers. On occasions other children would point toy guns at them, chanting, 'We're going to kill your family,' and laughing. It broke my heart to hear about it, and I wished I knew of a way to help them, to protect them from the taunting and the constant media coverage, but I couldn't. Hiding them from the world wasn't the answer. All I could do was listen to their worries, help them in any way I could and hope that this would blow over after a while. Time was the only thing that could help them, and they dealt with everything with a strength that continued to make me proud of them.

The constant pressures from the press got to the point that I ended up going to the police about it. 'Is there anything you can do?' I begged them. 'Anything to stop these people hounding me and my family?'

They were very kind, but I could tell by the look on their faces that they weren't going to be able to help me.

'There's really not much we *can* do,' I was told. 'Perhaps you should think about going away for a while, until things calm down a bit. Is there somewhere safe you can go to?'

I shook my head. 'There's nowhere,' I said quietly. And it was true. The only place where I would ever have sought sanctuary, the only place where I would ever have felt safe, was now a crime scene.

Those few days following the murders passed in a blur of misery. Half the time I hated Stuart for what he had done; half the time I was frantic to know that he was all right. And the pain of having lost Vicky was with me constantly. Simon and the children did their very best to keep me cheerful, but they were as shocked as I was, and the cloud that had descended over our house on that sunny Sunday did not leave.

It was a few days after the murders that Stuart first appeared in court. I watched on the television as his car approached the courtrooms. The windows were blacked out, but I found myself desperately trying to look through those windows to see if I could get any glimpse of him. A crowd of newsmen were gathered waiting to report on his arrival, and as the door of the car opened there was a barrage of camera flashes. I could not see Stuart's face because it was covered by a grey blanket – whether at his insistence or not I don't know – but I would have recognised him anywhere: the familiar gait, the tattoos on his forearms, the suntan he always had from working out of doors. For some reason it shocked me to see him handcuffed to a prison officer, but then I realised I was going to have to get used to images like that. My brother had committed a wicked crime, and society had a way of dealing with wicked criminals.

A few days later two policewomen came round to take a statement from me. It was a traumatic experience, but they were kind and supportive and with their help I got through it. At the end, I asked them a question that I had wanted to ask from the moment they arrived. 'How's Vicky's mum?'

The two policewomen looked serious. 'She's still unconscious,' one of them told me. 'She still doesn't know about her daughters' deaths.'

Somehow their words seemed to sum up the enormity of what Stuart had done. I closed my eyes as I thought about the awful moment when she would wake up and learn that Vicky and Emma were gone. I wondered how I would feel, being told that my daughters had been murdered. It didn't bear thinking about.

Just after the policewomen left, the phone rang. It had been ringing a lot over the last few days – friends, mostly, calling to check that we were all right – but each time it rang I had the strange sensation of thinking it would be Vicky calling, followed by the pang of realisation that actually Vicky would never call again. It was like being informed of her death twenty times a day. I picked it up with shaky hands. 'Hello.'

'Jayne, is that you?'

My breath stuck in my throat. It was Stuart.

I could barely speak for shock. He sounded so normal, as if the events of the previous weekend had never happened. As if it was just an ordinary phone call from a brother to his sister.

'Stu,' I replied. 'Oh my God, you can phone me?'

Words stuck in my throat. I wanted to ask him why. Why had he done this dreadful thing? But I did not trust myself to talk about Vicky. Strange though it sounds, and despite everything, I wanted to be a support to my brother, and I knew that if we started talking about Vicky all I would be able to show him was my anger. That was a conversation to be had face to face, not on the telephone.

'Jayne,' he said, 'I feel so bad for Jacqui. I hope she's all right. Blood pissed out everywhere when I shot her . . .'

I felt sickened to the pit of my stomach and tried to change the subject.

'Are the police looking after you, Stu?' I asked.

'Do you know what, Jayne?' he replied. 'This is the best the police have *ever* looked after me. Strange, isn't it?'

We chatted for maybe a minute about unimportant things. Finally Stuart said, 'Look, doll, I've got to go. You know I've always loved you, don't you? And I always will?'

'I love you too, Stu,' I replied in a small voice.

'Will you stick by me?'

'Of course I will.' And I put the phone down.

Stuart's phone call only added to my confusion. How could I stick by him? I, along with the rest of the country, despised him for what he had done; and yet I loved him at the same time.

I told Simon that Stuart had called. He sat down with me and held my hand. 'How did he sound?' he asked.

I shrugged sadly. 'Kind of normal,' I replied.

'And how did you feel? Talking to him, I mean.'

I thought about that for a while. 'I felt like I wanted to hate him, but I wanted to be there for him too.' And as I spoke, a realisation struck me. 'He's going to go to prison for a long time. I know that, and I know it's the right thing. But nothing they can do to him will ever be as bad as the things that'll be going on in his head when he thinks of what he did to Vicky. That's going to be the worst punishment of all, living with the truth of what he's done. He loved her.'

We sat in silence for a moment.

'I'm scared,' I said finally. 'Scared what Stuart will do to himself. I don't know if he'll be able to live with his crime, Simon. I don't know if he'll ever be able to live with it.'

I started to write a diary over this period – no dates, just a series of daily thoughts – and when I read it back now, I relive once more those agonising feelings of misery and doubt.

*Today I hurt as I have done every day since Sunday, 6 June. There are no changes to our pain; the loss of our beloved Vicky haunts us. I miss you, Vicky, so much. How will I ever cope without our friendship? How will I ever cope without your friendly voice? God, Vicky, I wish I could see you now and tell you just how much we love you, how perfect you are. Stuart: why, why, why? Why did you take these people's lives away? How could you do this? How can I still love you? I'm feeling so sad inside my heart. My God, it's only two days – I cannot even think of the next month, let alone the next year. Will our pain ever go?*

*Stuart, after all you have done, we all love you so much and miss you. I wish I could hate you even for just a moment. I just wish I could see you and give you a hug. I know you are probably so sorry, but even you know it's too late for sorry. You went too far. My poor Vicky.*

*I wish I could help my children. God help me, I am so weak. I worry for Vicky's mum – how will she ever cope knowing her daughters are no longer with her? It's so cruel, I don't understand this. Why?*

*Stuart telephoned me today. I was so excited to hear his voice. He sounded distant. Oh my God,*

*I am so worried for him. It's sick. He took my friend away
from me, and he took a mother and father's daughters
away. So much death. I cannot stop my feelings. I know it's
wrong to feel the way I do. Stuart, I so want to ask you why,
but I am afraid you will want to die again and selfishly I
don't want any more pain.*

*HELP. STOP THIS PAIN.*

*I don't want to write today. Just take the pain away from
my children and me. Please.*

After the first call, Stuart phoned me every two or three
days. The calls were short and always surprisingly ordinary.
I still could not bring myself to talk to him about Vicky,
preferring to do that face to face when the time came, and
I kept asking him to arrange a visiting order for me. On the
morning of Saturday, 19 June, when the children were all in
bed with me and Simon, the phone rang.

'Jayne, is that you?'

'Stuart! Are you OK?'

'Listen, Jayne,' my brother replied. 'I know it's a stupid
question, but are you all right?'

'Yeah, I'm all right, Stu,' I lied, trying to keep my voice
positive. 'What about you?'

'My head's like a shed,' he replied. 'I feel sick all the time.

Anyway, listen, I haven't got a lot of money on this card, so if it cuts out, sorry, OK?'

'OK.'

'I love you stacks, Jayne, and I've sorted it for you to come and visit me. You just have to have a police check first. You will come and see me, yeah?'

'Course I will, Stu. I can't wait, honestly.'

'Tuesday, then. You will come?' He sounded anxious.

'Stu, I won't let you down, I promise.'

'Good, because I've got something I have to tell you.'

I didn't know whether to be alarmed or intrigued. 'What is it, Stu? What have you got to tell me?'

'I can't tell you on the phone, Jayne. It's a secret. People might be listening in – we have to be careful what we say.' I suddenly became aware that he was sounding agitated and confused.

'All right, Stu,' I started to tell him. 'I promise I'll be there—'

But there was a click as his credit ran out, and he was gone.

For the rest of the day I was excited and apprehensive in equal measure about seeing Stuart. Part of me wished I had managed to persuade him to tell me what this great secret was, but at the same time I remembered the agitation in his voice and I consoled myself that, like talk of Vicky, it was something that would be best dealt with face to face.

Nevertheless I was anxious to know what it was he wanted to say, and I looked forward to the following Tuesday when I would finally be able to speak to my brother.

The following day, Sunday, was Simon's birthday. It dawned bright and sunny, much like that Sunday two weeks previously when all our lives had been for ever changed. Unlike then, however, the sunshine did not bring a smile to my face when I woke up at about seven o'clock in the morning. Like every day since the murders, the best I could hope for was that today would be a little bit better than the day before. Sometimes it was, sometimes it wasn't. You could never tell how it was going to be.

Normally for Simon's birthday I'd make a bit of fuss – balloons, cake, the sort of things designed more for the kids than for him, but which were fun for all of us too. Today, though, I could not bring myself to do all that. I think everybody understood. I think they felt the same. It being the weekend, the hounding from the press had eased off a little, but still we all carried a weight of anxiety on our shoulders; and my memory of that day is that from the moment I woke up I felt just a little bit more worried than I had during the days that preceded it. A bit strange. Perhaps it had been something unspoken in my conversation with Stuart; perhaps it was something else; perhaps I was just imagining it. Whatever the cause, I knew I had no chance of chasing away the numbness that had cloaked me for the past two weeks, no matter how much I wanted to make things ordinary for my family.

As the morning wore on, the more I felt that there was something ominous about today. I kept the feeling to myself and tried to shake it off, but I couldn't. It was with me whatever I tried to do. I told myself it was nothing. That I was imagining things.

A friend of ours came round to see us. We sat and drank tea and chatted. We talked about crimes of passion, and of Stuart, and of Vicky. We discussed the way they were with each other, how they acted as a couple; we even tried to have a laugh and a joke about their personalities, trying to remember some of the funny times – an attempt, I suppose, to recapture some happy memories from the quagmire of misery in which we found ourselves.

At around half-past three, the telephone rang. I was still chatting to our friend, so Simon answered, and I remember watching a flicker of confusion cross his face as he did so. Slowly he handed me the phone. 'It's your dad,' he said softly.

My brow furrowed. It was more than unusual for my father to call me. In fact, it was practically unheard of, and my first thoughts were of my mum. We had not spoken much since Vicky's death, but I knew that she too had been having a hard time of it with the press hounding her and pushing notes through the door day and night – all this, of course, on top of her worries about her son. I took the phone, slightly reluctantly.

'Hello, Dad.'

'Jayne.' His voice sounded gruff at the other end of the phone. Slightly out of breath. 'Is Simon there? Is he with you? Is he near you?'

'Course he is, Dad,' I replied, confused. 'You just spoke to him, didn't you?' Maybe it was my dad I should be worrying about, not my mum. Maybe his state of mind was fragile.

Suddenly he shouted. 'Right. Get him near you. Now!'

Extreme panic crashed over me. 'What is it, Dad? Is it Mum? Is she OK?'

'I said, get him close to you. Now!' And then the words that I sometimes think will ring in my head for as long as I live. 'Your brother's committed suicide.'

I dropped the phone.

All strength left my body.

I fell to the floor as though I had been physically hit.

I lay there, paralysed.

And then I screamed. An uncontrollable, inhuman scream that echoed around the house and, for all I know, down the street. I felt my nails scratch against the wooden floor and my stomach cramped up as though somebody had roughly clenched it. Everything around me seemed to happen in slow motion: I became aware of my children, crying hysterically at the sight of their mother collapsed on the floor, but not knowing what it was that had dealt her this devastating blow; the friend taking them away; Simon, there for me as always, but not knowing how to deal with my sudden deterioration.

I screamed and I screamed and I screamed. 'No! Stuart! No!' My head was going to burst. I wanted to die.

My nails were bleeding now from scratching maniacally at the floor. My vision was blurred. There were people all around me trying to comfort me in my hour of need, but nobody could say anything to dispel the agonising despair.

My sobs continued to overcome my body. I would never have thought I had as many tears in me as I cried that day. When my babies were brought back into the house they simply stood in front of me, silent, as they watched me rocking from side to side and wailing with an unspeakable grief.

At first I refused to believe it. I refused to believe that life could have dealt me yet another intolerable blow. First Graham, then Vicky, now Stuart – how much could one person be expected to take? How much more could life hurl at me? As I did on the night Vicky died, I started trying to find some other explanation. He had been murdered; the prison had neglected him. There was certainly no way he had committed suicide. I had only spoken to him yesterday. He had said he had something to tell me. Something secret. He would not have taken his own life without seeing me and concluding that piece of unfinished business, whatever it was.

On the afternoon of Stuart's death, I started putting a series of increasingly strong and accusatory calls through to the prison, demanding to know what had happened and also demanding that I come and see him right then. Of course, that was never going to happen, and I tormented myself with visions of him lying in a cold morgue, all alone. In my mind, I pictured his soul floating above him, looking down and seeing that there was nobody with him. I couldn't bear that.

My despair became anger, which in turn became a brooding numbness. I felt such empty desolation, such bitter hatred for the world and everything in it, that I could barely function.

Only gradually did I allow the truth to sink in.

Vicky was dead – darling Vicky, whom I loved like a sister. And now Stuart, my beloved, flawed, monstrous brother, the man I adored and despised in equal measure, had been destroyed by the demons that I had watched growing in him for years.

My grief was all-consuming and of a nature that I could not explain to anyone around me. My pain was not just psychological, but physical – a tangible agony that I felt would never leave me. How much more could happen to one family? How much guilt was I supposed to be able to bear?

I found myself unable to articulate a single word, unable to speak even to the loved ones around me.

I knew that my life could not possibly get any worse.


The world did not mourn my brother, nor did I expect it to. To everyone else he was evil. A murderer. He had killed two young women in the prime of their lives; he had robbed a mother of her daughters in a fashion so brutal that it did not bear thinking about. The world thought he was a monster. The world was right.

But he was still my brother. He was still the little boy who loved and protected me. He was still the man who had been driven to distraction, maybe even to desperation, by my refusal to let him seek revenge for what had happened to me as a little girl. Despite everything, even in death – especially in death – I still loved him. When I had spoken to him for the last time, I had made a promise. I had said I would go and see him. I had said I would stand by him. I did not intend to go back on that promise. It was the only thing left that I could do for him.

Tuesday, 22 June 2004 was supposed to be the day I was to visit Stuart in prison; as it turned out, it was the day that

I made the journey to a soulless hospital in Milton Keynes to view his body. Simon arranged for the children to be looked after so that he could be with me, to support me at this most difficult time, and Simon's sister, Michelle, and her husband, Hector, kindly agreed to drive us.

I will never forget that journey. Just before we got into the car, I turned to Simon and said, 'I don't know if I can go through with this.'

He held me tight. 'I think you'll regret it if you don't,' he said.

'Why didn't he just wait for me?' I asked, half to Simon, half to myself. 'Why didn't he just wait for me to see him? Maybe I could have done something . . .'

Simon didn't reply.

'We have to go, don't we?' I asked.

'Yes,' he replied quietly. 'It's time.'

We climbed into the waiting car. Michelle sat next to me, took my hand, and we embarked upon the all-too-long, all-too-short journey to Milton Keynes. It was late afternoon when we set off; just before six p.m. we were at the hospital. We waited at the front desk as we had been instructed to do.

'Mrs Sterne?' A smart lady with a soft voice approached us.

'Yes,' I replied. 'Hello. Thank you for letting me see my brother.'

She smiled gently at me. 'You're welcome,' she said, and

asked us to follow her. 'They're just finishing off getting him ready now,' she told me. 'They've done a very good job of cleaning him up.'

I shuddered at the implication of what she had just said.

We arrived at an office, and were offered a seat. The lady introduced herself properly as being the coroner. She briefly told us what her job entailed – to be honest I didn't take much of it in – before asking me a question. 'Would you like to know the details of how your brother died?'

I had not prepared myself for this, and for a moment did not know how to answer. Half of me was desperate to learn every detail I possibly could; the other half of me simply wanted to run from the room. But I found myself nodding slowly.

The coroner nodded in reply. 'Stuart was determined to take his life,' she told us, 'but I have to tell you that there are many quicker and easier ways to die than the one he chose.'

And then she explained to me what had happened.

*In my mind's eye, I will forever see him, sitting in his little cell. It is sometime after 9.05 a.m. He has just been given some medication and has requested two razor blades. He sits on his bed. He remembers Vicky. Perhaps he cries. Certainly he hates himself and what he has done. He knows he has become a monster.*

*Slowly, he takes a razor blade. He draws a deep breath, and then slices himself along one side of his neck. Blood seeps from the* cut. A second slash. A third. And then he does the same on the other side of his neck.

Blood is pumping from him now. He stands up and walks around the cell. His pulse is strong, and it forces the blood to splash against the walls and over the floor. After a few minutes the place looks like a bloodbath. But Stuart is still alive. Still walking. Still bleeding. Still hurting inside. According to the doctors, he remains like this for forty-five minutes.

My brother does not understand why he is not dead. He takes a shoelace from his shoe. Weak now, and fumbling, he ties it around his neck. He attaches the other end to the base of his bed. Then he slumps down, pulling the whole of his considerable body weight down against the shoelace, which by now is saturated with his blood. The shoelace tugs against his bleeding neck, and soon he loses consciousness.

At 11.15 a.m. a prison chaplain looks through the hatch in his door. He sees a lot of blood and raises the alarm.

Attempts are made to revive Stuart, but it is far too late and my brother was too determined to die.

At 11.54 a.m., he is pronounced dead.


'Are there any other questions you want to ask?'

'No,' I replied. What could I possibly ask after hearing all that?

A man walked into the room and informed us that Stuart was ready. It was all so unreal as I took Simon by the hand

and was led to the place where my brother lay. The door to the room opened, and I froze.

The room was stark and bare; it had a smell about it that I did not recognise. And Stuart was there, lying under a blanket, still and silent. He didn't look dead. Just asleep. I remembered the time he had fallen asleep while sitting on the cold floor of his bedroom holding my hand. He looked no different to that, really.

Nervously I stepped into the room and approached him. The wounds on his neck, which had previously been gaping wide, had been expertly glued up and didn't look nearly as bad as I expected them too. He had been given a change of clothes, of course, because the garments he was wearing during his final moments were saturated with blood. I looked closer at his face. There was a small amount of bruising around his cheeks, but apart from that he looked just as he had done in life. He looked almost peaceful, and as I stared at him, I felt overwhelmed with a flood of memories.

I remembered the little boy who was bullied in Ireland; I remembered the way he stood up to them, the way he learnt to defend himself and the way he developed a taste for fighting. I remembered the day he walked in to see Graham beating me with a wet towel, and the retribution that followed. I remembered the day he brought Vicky to meet me, and the irrepressible, childish smile he had on his face. I remembered how happy they were together. I remembered the awful night when I told Stuart of Graham's abuse, and the pain and anguish in his voice. I remembered how he went downhill after that, lost in a fog of alcohol and self-loathing.

I remembered when I first learned what he had done. I remembered him asking me to forgive him. To forgive the unforgivable. Could I ever do that? I simply didn't know.

I bent down and kissed my brother. I knew that dead bodies were cold, but nothing could have prepared me for the sheer iciness of his skin. I couldn't understand it, because he looked so warm; I pulled the blanket gently a bit further up his body.

It relieved me that he looked so peaceful. There was no anguish in his face. No hate. No self-loathing. He had gone to a place where his dreadful actions could no longer haunt him. And though they would continue to haunt others for many years to come, I felt, selfishly, pleased that my brother's personal torment had ended.

I smiled. It was the first time I had smiled in a long time. Now, I knew, I could say goodbye. There would be a funeral, of course. I would follow his coffin, and read some heartfelt words. I would try and keep away from the unseemly prying of the newspaper lenses. I would cry. But the real goodbye was to be said here, now, in this cold, uninviting hospital room. Just me and him.

'Stuart,' I whispered to him, 'I love you so much. I'm so sorry you felt so sad and so alone.' And I kissed his cold skin again, for the final time. Then I turned to Simon. 'We can go now,' I told him. 'I've done what I came to do, and the children will want us back.'

He put his arm round me and we turned to leave, closing the door quietly behind us.

# Epilogue

When Stuart's death was announced, the whole country seemed to feel that the world was a better place without him. No doubt they are right. His monstrous actions were vile, and for right-thinking people they can never be condoned. They can certainly never be excused.

But they can, perhaps, be explained.

Children are not born evil, but they can be damaged. I know that better than most. When Graham first laid his hands on me all those years ago, he did more than damage my childhood. He destroyed it. And though I have learned to accept what happened, to come to terms with it, to live with it, barely a day goes by when I do not remember the torment to which he subjected me. In my darkest nightmares I remember the thumping beat of 'Almost Human', and I am playing Jackie with him once again. I know those memories will be with me until my dying day, and though I have accepted what happened, sometimes I cannot help but weep at the thought of that defenceless little girl in the clutches of such a monster.

One of the worst things about being abused is the sense of loneliness. You want to tell everybody, yet you cannot tell anyone for fear of being thought bad or naughty. It is a solitary, miserable way to grow up. And despite everything that followed, I know that had it not been for the care and love of my brother Stuart, the path that I finally trod could have been very different. Even now, after all that he has done, I cannot help but remember the little boy who comforted me, and the teenager who protected my honour.

One thing haunts me more than any other. In my heart of hearts, I truly believe that if I had never told Stuart about the way I was abused as a child, he would never have pushed himself over the edge. Despite what he finally did, he had a very personal sense of justice, and it angered him deeply that I would not let him avenge the brutality I underwent. It more than angered him: it shamed him, and I believe he could not cope with that shame in his life. You cannot change the past, and I still think that stopping him going to Graham was the right thing to do, but almost daily I reflect upon one fact: Graham's abuse did not only destroy my life, it destroyed the lives of many others. Hard though it might be, I can try to forgive Stuart; but I can never forgive what my abuser did to me and, indirectly, to others.

I will always live in the shadow of the past. How can I not? But sometimes you have to stop looking back. You have to gaze around you, appreciate what you have, and start looking forwards. I have much to be thankful for. I have a wonderful partner, and four beautiful children. My eldest, Emma, now has a daughter of her own. Now my family brings me intense, searing joy – not sadness.

They say that when you reach rock bottom, the only way is up. I am discovering that this is true. And I know now that I have a purpose in life – to tell my story in the hope that my experiences will help others. If my history can stop just one child going through what I did, I will feel that, in some small way, my suffering has been vindicated.

If I have learned anything from these dreadful events it is this: even if the past cannot be changed, the future can. I will continue to give my own children the love, protection and kindness that they deserve. And when the time comes for them to have families of their own, I hope that they will do the same, because I know only too well what can happen when those essential gifts that every adult can give are taken away.

# Acknowledgements

To Simon, my husband and best friend. Thank you for being so patient, so loving and so supportive. Over the many times I struggled, you raised your abilities to cope on a level beyond your own expectations. Thank you for the encouragement and guidance you gave me during the times that I wanted to give up. Thank you for giving me hope, inspiration and faith that I could make this book possible. Thank you for simply being you.

To my four wonderful children, Emma, Luke, Bethany and Alyce. You are all so brave, beautiful and clever. You have all made the dullest of days seem brighter and have shown immense courage during our time of pain and sorrow. I love you all so much. You have reached a loving understanding of one another, supporting each other during the most difficult times. Your thoughtful ways have given me the strength to see beyond my own pain and to look at the positives that I have in my life. You have shown wisdom, kindness and unity, and I feel immensely proud of you all.

To my parents and my sister, thank you for your support. Mum, I think you are an amazing woman; I'm proud to have you as my mother, and I love you very much. Dad, I am so proud to be your daughter and love you very much.

To Yeewan and Duncan, Kerry, Jon and Sue, Michelle and Hector, Jason, Mick and Irene, Andy, Terry, Gavin, Symond and Tom Hendry – thank you for sharing your time with me and allowing me to laugh and cry. Your patience and help through the darkest moments I have encountered during my grief have been a huge support.

To the old gang from High Wycombe, thank you for contacting me and simply being a comfort. I can't find the words to express how lucky I feel to have such a good network of friends.

Thanks to Robert Smith, my agent, Adam Parfitt, who helped turn my feelings into words, and a special thank you goes to Carly Cook, my brilliant editor – three amazing people driven by determination, compassion and hard work. You believed in my book from the very start and your enthusiasm was infectious. I will always be grateful for your kind words and the friendship I feel I have gained with you all. Thank you.

*More Non-fiction from Headline Review*

# DADDY'S LITTLE GIRL

## Julia Latchem-Smith

Julia's family was a picture of respectability. To the outside world it was middle class, decent, loving. But her mother didn't love her enough. And her father loved her too much.

Between the ages of eight and thirteen, Julia's father sexually abused her. Loyal to her family, and desperate to keep it intact, the abuse had to become their little secret. Even as Julia struggled to come to terms with her ordeal, she knew that revealing the truth would rip her family apart.

When she finally cried out for help, she was encouraged to retract her allegations and branded a liar. In her teenage years, she began to doubt her own sanity. Had the abuse really happened? Her father couldn't have done that . . . could he?

This is the harrowing story of how Julia's father abused her trust, and cheated her of her childhood. But it is also the uplifting story of how, years later, Julia successfully confronted her painful past and began to carve out for herself a meaningful future.

**NON-FICTION / MEMOIR 978 0 7553 1638 0**